# Departures

# Departures

Poems & Meditations on the Book of Exodus

*P. D. GRAY*

RESOURCE *Publications* • Eugene, Oregon

DEPARTURES
Poems & Meditations on the Book of Exodus

Copyright © 2020 P. D. Gray. All rights reserved. Except for brief quotations in critical publications or reviews, no part of this book may be reproduced in any manner without prior written permission from the publisher. Write: Permissions, Wipf and Stock Publishers, 199 W. 8th Ave., Suite 3, Eugene, OR 97401.

Resource Publications
An Imprint of Wipf and Stock Publishers
199 W. 8th Ave., Suite 3
Eugene, OR 97401

www.wipfandstock.com

PAPERBACK ISBN: 978-1-7252-6481-6
HARDCOVER ISBN: 978-1-7252-6482-3
EBOOK ISBN: 978-1-7252-6483-0

Manufactured in the U.S.A.    03/24/20

As well as my parents, who have always supported me in everything I have shown an interest in, and my wife who has loved me since we were drawn together by God, I would also like to dedicate this book to the memory of Pastor Henry Mahan, whose audio sermons were used providentially to bring me to that blessed state of assurance of salvation in Christ alone. I would also like to express much gratitude to Dr. Peter Masters, whose teaching has helped shape and mold me in my walk with the Lord, as I seek to be sanctified by the ongoing work of the Holy Spirit.

Now all these things happened unto them for ensamples: and they are written for our admonition, upon whom the ends of the world are come.

—1 Corinthians 10:11

# Contents

Author's Note | ix
Exodus 1 | 1
Exodus 2 | 5
Exodus 3 | 8
Exodus 4 | 11
Exodus 5 | 16
Exodus 6 | 20
Exodus 7 | 24
Exodus 8 | 28
Exodus 9 | 32
Exodus 10 | 36
Exodus 11 | 40
Exodus 12 | 45
Exodus 13 | 50
Exodus 14 | 54
Exodus 15 | 58
Exodus 16 | 62
Exodus 17 | 66
Exodus 18 | 72
Exodus 19 | 77
Exodus 20 | 82
Exodus 21 | 86
Exodus 22 | 91
Exodus 23 | 96
Exodus 24 | 101
Exodus 25 | 105
Exodus 26 | 111
Exodus 27 | 115
Exodus 28 | 120
Exodus 29 | 125
Exodus 30 | 130
Exodus 31 | 135
Exodus 32 | 140
Exodus 33 | 145
Exodus 34 | 151
Exodus 35 | 155
Exodus 36 | 160
Exodus 37 | 165
Exodus 38 | 170
Exodus 39 | 175
Exodus 40 | 179

# Author's Note

WHILST REVIEWING THE BOOK of Exodus I have felt myself a wonderer and reflector upon something of the depth, breadth, and inter-connectedness of the Scriptures, as together they speak as one infallible, authoritative Holy Word. I believe that the seed of this book was planted during a series of sermons preached by Dr. Peter Masters at the Metropolitan Tabernacle in 2014, which I found to be most instructive and helpful.

It would be my advice for you first to read and deeply reflect upon each chapter of Exodus in turn, dipping into a tried and tested commentary such as that of Gill, Henry, or Poole. I would then advise you to read each successive meditation and poem whilst prayerfully consulting the various verses which I believe can relate to and shed light upon the particular chapter in question. This book is designed as a devotional aid, not a scholarly commentary.

Augustine's 'the Old is the New concealed, the New the Old revealed' is worth holding to, in order that we do not unnecessarily restrict or straitjacket any part of Scripture from the rest of divinely revealed truth. Like the harmonics of just one note on a piano, the Christian who wishes to "grow in grace, and *in* the knowledge of our Lord and Savior Jesus Christ" (2 Pet 3:18) would do well to become a spiritual piano tuner, one who feels the vast range of other notes which reverberate in any given note on the divine keyboard, so to speak.

I have profited much from reading A. W. Pink's 'Gleanings in Exodus', and have used it to help me stumble my way through this mighty, majestic second book of the Bible. Aside from a few dispensational leanings and numerical obsessions which were progressively purged out during his earthly pilgrimage, nearly all of Pink's concise and insightful writings are well worth reading. His work is exacting and succinct, most suitable for our modern age.

## Author's Note

I have also learned from Henry Mahan's 'With New Testament Eyes' to see the Old Testament as a place from which much spiritual treasure can be mined as it foretells, typifies, and magnifies so many facets of our Lord and Savior Jesus Christ. May this modest volume lead each one of us to glorify God and be a blessing to others, as we seek to progress along that divinely ordained narrow way.

P. D. Gray

# Exodus 1

God's dealings with the midwives as with so many things in the Old Testament are instructive for the modern-day Christian. They were blessed because they were elect persons of faith, trustees of the deliverance to come through the promised Seed. They "feared God", no doubt recognizing the handiwork of the devil working through "the king of Egypt" (v.17) whom they disobeyed. Rendered 100% righteous in advance through the perfect obedience of the Messiah to come, their own personal obedience was on that journey of faith; imperfect, flawed, learning every day.

And so the midwives said unto Pharaoh, "Because the Hebrew women *are* not as the Egyptian women; for they *are* lively, and are delivered ere the midwives come in unto them" (v.19). In His omniscient justice, every slight distortion, called by the world a 'white lie', is abhorred by God. But what if they *had* outright defied Pharaoh to his face? Well, God surely would have made that the way for His perfect plan to have been fulfilled, the midwives receiving the commensurate honor ordained for them before time began. As it happened, a more (though not entirely) perfect obedience would be exemplified by Moses as a type of Christ.

Let us look then into our own lives and see how far we are actually, daily measuring up to the high and holy standard lived out by our perfect, righteous Representative. Oh how much we yearn to do better; how grateful we are to be viewed not in the flesh but in Christ: "Therefore God dealt well with the midwives: and the people multiplied, and waxed very mighty. And it came to pass, because the midwives feared God, that he made them houses" (v.20–21). Who among us has not received multitudinous blessings in the Spirit despite our faltering, flickering obedience towards His holy law?

A believer in the woman's Seed now finds comfort in the company of believers, the pages of Scripture, the relief and respite of prayer. Such a one can no longer walk in a worldly way, or at least not without remorse and repentance, for "If we say that we have fellowship with him, and walk in darkness, we lie, and do not the truth" (1 John 1:6). A Christian is one who has fallen out of love with the world, the flesh, the devil, and now seeks albeit imperfectly to walk with God: "But if we walk in the light, as he is in the light, we have fellowship one with another, and the blood of Jesus Christ his Son cleanseth us from all sin" (v.7). May we look therefore with the midwives beyond Moses to our perfect Mediator, for He not only awaits us but walks with us every day.

# Exodus 1

## VERSES UPON WHICH TO MEDITATE

*(ideally in each chapter's context)*

### *1 John 1:6–7*

If we say that we have fellowship with him, and walk in darkness, we lie, and do not the truth:

But if we walk in the light, as he is in the light, we have fellowship one with another, and the blood of Jesus Christ his Son cleanseth us from all sin.

**We Midwives**

In slavery we toil and strive
believing that we are alive,
while all the while taskmasters trick
adding to bondage, mortar, brick.

In darkness do we sleep and rise
these worldly plans to realize,
though there are feelings in the wings
midwives of faith our Father brings.

And so we're sought and so we pray
Satan commands, must we obey?
our hearts reveal our desperate need
God buries us in holy Seed.

The devil's strength tests our resolve
though in the Seed we rise, revolve,
our sins and Pharaoh drag out days
thank God we're cleansed in Risen's rays.

# Exodus 2

THERE ARE SOME REMARKABLE things about Exodus 2. Firstly, the extent to which Hebrews 11 complements and completes it. Into Exodus 2:10 Hebrews 11:24–27 perfectly slots and explains to us the miraculous conversion of a younger Moses, encapsulating the spiritual growth of his formative years. Thus it is that Scripture best interprets Scripture, and so it is that none of us but by the Holy Spirit would have had any spiritual interest, enslaved by and willfully enslaving ourselves to the pharaohs of this vainglorious world.

Second, there is the remarkable reality that Moses had, humanly speaking, nothing to gain and so very much to lose by his turning away from the exalted privilege of being an adopted member of the Egyptian royal family of that time. Like being a member of the British royal family of today or the son of a US President, to turn one's back on all the the pyramids of wealth, spheres of political influence, exalted spires of learning and all manner of other benefits, is unthinkable. Coming from my background it is not something with which I can empathize and I can only imagine the frenzied depths of Satanic opposition to it.

And yet by God's powerful work deep in Moses' heart, he was graciously granted the power to refuse (Heb 11:24), to consciously choose "to suffer affliction" (v.25), to thoughtfully esteem "the reproach of Christ" (v.26), to forsake all worldly privilege whilst "not fearing the wrath of the king" (v.27), and by faith to see "him who is invisible" (v.27).

Such a remarkable miracle is a localized type of the miracles occurring globally in our New Testament age. Who among us would have ever turned away from powerful worldly attractions and idolatrous aspirations were it not for the divine operation at work within? Like Moses we reject all human glory and attribute everything to our Father in heaven who was responsible for having drawn us out by grace, else all had gone most horribly astray.

## VERSES UPON WHICH TO MEDITATE

*(ideally in each chapter's context)*

### Hebrews 11:24-27

By faith Moses, when he was come to years, refused to be called the son of Pharaoh's daughter;

Choosing rather to suffer affliction with the people of God, than to enjoy the pleasures of sin for a season;

Esteeming the reproach of Christ greater riches than the treasures in Egypt: for he had respect unto the recompence of the reward.

By faith he forsook Egypt, not fearing the wrath of the king: for he endured, as seeing him who is invisible.

**The Miracle Within**

So *Moses* was the name she called
as if to make her baby claimed,
though Moses grew to be appalled
by lies the mummy's ties proclaimed.

Sin's haunts arose as pyramids
alluring Moses, brick by brick,
though grace through faith sees through eyelids
released within from Satan's trick.

He looked unto the world's Messiah
next to whom Pharaoh was dust,
he felt within a holy fire
scouring sin as so much rust.

And now to brethren did he turn
entombing evil in the sand,
yet all the called ones will not learn
until God's Son they under stand.

# Exodus 3

It is interesting and instructive to see the ways in which Moses doubted self and questioned God, for if it were just one fleeting doubt we would not be able to relate. In our lives as Christians there are small and sometimes big moments at which our faith fails us and we are brought to the end of self, not all at once but through the inward turbulence of thoughts and emotions. We learn to lean upon the outward word of God, strangely kindled by the inward motions of the Holy Spirit. It can be a period of wrestling at the end of which we become spiritually stronger and further weaned from wretched, moribund self.

How utterly 'other' is our holy "I AM" to everything upon which this world's cruel, doomed structures lie. Lest we be tempted to be over-critical of Moses we must remember that he was living in his present, just as we are living in ours. Were someone to look back at the preserved narrative of *our* lives in thousands of years' time, how would it fare with us? Our Lord is inextricably bound up in all that we are and do; He is ever present and everlasting and with Him is no beginning nor end. While this world, "Egypt", may fret about its depleting resources, its waning environment, its insecure strength and ever-shifting rights, God's kingdom, "Israel", is brought to surrender to "I AM", for in Him it has all that it needs.

There is sadly also, in the "jewels of gold" (v.22), an ominous foreshadowing of that terrible and tragic fall from grace exemplified by the false worship of the molten calf. When the Lord loads the professing church of Christ with benefits and material provision, how sad that these things can become a snare. May we like Moses value Jesus more each day, so much more than "the treasures in Egypt" (Heb 11:26). In a solemn aloneness may we commit our selves afresh to the holy "I AM", trusting not our hearts, remembering how "our fathers would not obey, but thrust" God's servant "from them, and in their hearts turned back again into Egypt" (Acts 7:39).

# Exodus 3

## VERSES UPON WHICH TO MEDITATE

*(ideally in each chapter's context)*

### Acts 7:39

To whom our fathers would not obey, but thrust *him* from them, and in their hearts turned back again into Egypt,

### Hebrews 11:26

Esteeming the reproach of Christ greater riches than the treasures in Egypt: for he had respect unto the recompence of the reward.

## God's Servant—Called

From fear the face of Moses hid
from God who had His servant bid,
bare-footed Moses heard God's voice,
a chosen man by grace not choice.

Then Moses uttered, 'Who am I'?
like us a sinner born to die,
but God assured him that he could,
because He sent—by faith he stood.

Still Moses—human—did persist,
so often do our hearts resist,
then all his doubts dissolved—I AM
not in himself but through I AM.

We learn that Moses esteemed Christ
forsaking Egypt, falsely priced,
how sad that gracious golden jewels
bestowed by God made many fools.

# Exodus 4

As well as the remarkable longsuffering of the Lord towards an all too human, excuse-laden Moses in Exodus 4, the specificity of the call is interesting. It was Moses specifically, and Aaron, who would be called on this mighty mission to lead the Israelites out of slavery at that moment in time. However, of those who "bowed their heads and worshipped" (4:31), it would turn out that not all Israel *were* Israel in that true, redemptive sense, theologically explicated in Romans 2. Lest a nation, any nation become puffed up and proud the Lord records for our instruction His particular, man-humbling creation of a people "formed" (Rom 9:20) as a "vessel unto honour" (v.21), intended chiefly for His glory and pleasure; our highest calling to be in and even used by His hand.

The argument is expounded in Isaiah 43 in which spiritual Israel is described as having been specifically made by God to be His possession: "O Israel, Fear not: for I have redeemed thee, I have called *thee* by thy name; thou *art* mine" (v.1). Moreover, such a people are to be brought "from the east, and . . . from the west" (v.5), from "the north" and "the south" (v.6); in other words, a global people. Even though God in Exodus 4 is seen threading a people through the limited fabric of theocratic Israel by the literal mouthpiece of Moses and Aaron, the vision is far grander and more comprehensive than might at first appear: "In the LORD shall all the seed of Israel be justified, and shall glory" (Isa 45:25).

Not that any saved-sinner is worthy of such a high and holy calling. Far from it, for despite having been "formed" for our Father's glory, we have "wearied" Him with our "iniquities" (Isa 43:24). Nevertheless, the good news of the gospel of salvation through Jesus Christ "the Holy One of Israel" (v.3) is that "I, even I, am he that blotteth out thy transgressions for mine own sake, and will not remember thy sins" (v.25). What cause for thanksgiving, repentance, and praise, especially at a time when Santa has all but eclipsed Christ in the popular imagination of the West. Let our mouths thus echo that "new song before the throne", sung by that symbolic number (Rev 14:3) as we millions dwell "as the stars of the heaven, and as the sand which *is* upon the sea shore" (Gen 22:17).

# Exodus 4

## VERSES UPON WHICH TO MEDITATE

*(ideally in each chapter's context)*

### Genesis 22:17

That in blessing I will bless thee, and in multiplying I will multiply thy seed as the stars of the heaven, and as the sand which *is* upon the sea shore; and thy seed shall possess the gate of his enemies;

### Isaiah 43:1, 3, 5-6, 24-25

But now thus saith the LORD that created thee, O Jacob, and he that formed thee, O Israel, Fear not: for I have redeemed thee, I have called *thee* by thy name; thou *art* mine.

For I *am* the LORD thy God, the Holy One of Israel, thy Saviour: I gave Egypt *for* thy ransom, Ethiopia and Seba for thee.

Fear not: for I *am* with thee: I will bring thy seed from the east, and gather thee from the west;

I will say to the north, Give up; and to the south, Keep not back: bring my sons from far, and my daughters from the ends of the earth;

Thou hast bought me no sweet cane with money, neither hast thou filled me with the fat of thy sacrifices: but thou hast made me to serve with thy sins, thou hast wearied me with thine iniquities.

I, *even* I, *am* he that blotteth out thy transgressions for mine own sake, and will not remember thy sins.

### 45:25

In the LORD shall all the seed of Israel be justified, and shall glory.

## *Romans 2:28-29*

For he is not a Jew, which is one outwardly; neither *is that* circumcision, which is outward in the flesh:

But he *is* a Jew, which is one inwardly; and circumcision *is that* of the heart, in the spirit, *and* not in the letter; whose praise *is* not of men, but of God.

## *9:20-21*

Nay but, O man, who art thou that repliest against God? Shall the thing formed say to him that formed *it*, Why hast thou made me thus?

Hath not the potter power over the clay, of the same lump to make one vessel unto honour, and another unto dishonour?

## *Revelation 14:3*

And they sung as it were a new song before the throne, and before the four beasts, and the elders: and no man could learn that song but the hundred *and* forty *and* four thousand, which were redeemed from the earth.

## Who Hath Made Man's Mouth?

The hand and heart and head of shame
were what the Lord with Moses dealt,
and so the rod a snake became
to show on what man's strength has dwelt.

The heart and head and hand of sin
exposed in Moses' very breast,
a leper, each of us within
without the One in whom we rest.

The head and hand and heart corrupt
as Moses trusted in his lips,
but God does ever man disrupt
employing words to man eclipse.

The hand and heart and head of pride
are what the Lord with us must quell,
our debt of sin can't be denied
a Substitute must take our hell.

# Exodus 5

MOST OF THE TIME, thank the Lord, it is possible for called-out church and blind-drunk world to dwell in relative peace and harmony in things temporal. If the world wants believers to jump over hurdles this high, go through hoops that wide, wear such and such a uniform or whatever else it may be, there is flexibility and liberty to allow it; true religion, after all, is an unshackling from the trappings of tradition, pride, and ceremony. Believers may rest easy in one sense, in that they are no longer setting their hearts upon the fading things of this vain and passing world.

There are times, however, when the believer must take a stand; not due to being difficult but because the burden of the Lord upon the heart outweighs the petty burdens of time and money. Then, as promised, our Shepherd will guide us past the menacing threat which may loom so large in the moment but years later seem pathetic and puny. Pharaoh's willful ignorance of God is revealed in his "Who *is* the LORD . . . ?" (Exod 5:2), before his monstrous love of power and money rears its ugly head: "Wherefore do ye, Moses and Aaron, let the people from their works?" (v.4), it being inconceivable to a worldling that the interests of money and time could ever play second fiddle to the spiritual things of church and chapel in "the wilderness" (v.1).

The believer, however, sees not a worldly wilderness but a spiritual "feast unto me in the wilderness" (v.1). It is not just that one has been liberated from the fatal corruptions of trespass, temptation, and treachery, such thieves as spiritually speaking "steal" and "kill" and "destroy" (John 10:10); it is that in the supernatural Seed alone the believer's heart is satisfied, circumcised, opened to have "life . . . more abundantly" (v.10) than before. Surrounded by fears, doubts, and enemies though we may be, nevertheless "Thou preparest a table before me in the presence of mine enemies: thou anointest my head with oil; my cup runneth over" (Ps 23:5).

A most beautiful song of praise and adoration will come in due course (Exod 15) but for now Moses' struggle to conquer himself, let alone Egypt, is a source of much comfort to us as we navigate through our generation's slave-built pyramids, refreshed from the pulpit along our pilgrim way.

## VERSES UPON WHICH TO MEDITATE

*(ideally in each chapter's context)*

### *Psalm 23:5*

Thou preparest a table before me in the presence of mine enemies: thou anointest my head with oil; my cup runneth over.

### *John 10:10*

The thief cometh not, but for to steal, and to kill, and to destroy: I am come that they might have life, and that they might have *it* more abundantly.

**Feast in the Wilderness**


When Moses, Aaron, Pharaoh met
this 'king' denied their strange request,
for worldly children will not let
God's children be, on holy quest.

Their burdens even were increased
no pilgrim journey was allowed,
their daily means cruelly decreased
new fears and doubts uttered aloud.

Thus Moses went unto the LORD,
poured out his heart in privacy,
God hears all prayers and does reward
His Christ-bound sheep, in secrecy.

The world deems Christians worthless, idle
pharaohs rule us still today,
the name of God still makes them bridle
—angels feast when sinners pray.

# Exodus 6

ONE DOESN'T NEED TO (but should) read the magnificent 'The Bondage of the Will' by Martin Luther, to know that we have a problem with our will, before and after conversion. Before conversion we fluctuate from loving to despising our sins but seem to have no alternative to the inevitability of them and so submit to them, "dead in trespasses and sins" (Eph 2:1) as we are. Pride stops us from seeking repentance while self-righteousness blocks faith from melting the heart; we are enslaved to our depraved, fallen wills and are in denial of this most terrible malady ("They that are whole have no need of the physician, but they that are sick" Mark 2:17).

The breaking of this bondage brings us into the promised land of walking by grace through faith in Jesus Christ; happy the day when we first come to the consciousness of it. Yet for the rest of our lives the challenge is to adopt the servanthood that should rightly characterize our renewed, restored relationship with our Master. This is no easy task but a lifelong series of challenges and God-given trials. It can clearly be seen in this sixth chapter, in which we may empathize with Moses' struggle to bring his life into alignment with the eternal promises of the Almighty. To God's "shalt" (v.1), His appeal to His covenantal relationship ("JEHOVAH" v.3), and His essential Godhood ("I *am* the LORD" v.7), Moses responds with doubt ("how then shall Pharaoh hear me . . . v.12) and discouragement (. . . who *am* of uncircumcised lips?" v.12).

There is a godly passivity and activity, and then there is an *ungodly* passivity and activity. We are reminded in John 15 that we are to obediently "Abide" in Christ (v.4) without whom we can "do nothing" (v.5) of any worth in God's sight. Equally, we can do "many" apparently "wonderful works" (Matt 7:22) in the name of Christ but they might actually be adding to the judgement of our souls and be viewed as "iniquity" (v.23) in the end! Moses' genuine faltering, his humble self-questioning and disappointing lack of active faith was, we must remember, conveyed through *his* pen under the inspiration of the Holy Spirit. These things are of much comfort and assurance to us, us who may be striving to live in a godly way as we wend our way through this dark world. May we not be discouraged for we have a God of patience and long-suffering who loves us and is on our side: "For which cause we faint not; but though our outward man perish, yet the inward *man* is renewed day by day" (2 Cor 4:16).

## VERSES UPON WHICH TO MEDITATE

*(ideally in each chapter's context)*

### *Matthew 7:22, 23*

Many will say to me in that day, Lord, Lord, have we not prophesied in thy name? and in thy name have cast out devils? and in thy name done many wonderful works?

And then will I profess unto them, I never knew you: depart from me, ye that work iniquity.

### *Mark 2:17*

When Jesus heard *it*, he saith unto them, They that are whole have no need of the physician, but they that are sick: I came not to call the righteous, but sinners to repentance.

### *John 15:4, 5*

Abide in me, and I in you. As the branch cannot bear fruit of itself, except it abide in the vine; no more can ye, except ye abide in me.

I am the vine, ye *are* the branches: He that abideth in me, and I in him, the same bringeth forth much fruit: for without me ye can do nothing.

### *2 Corinthians 4:16*

For which cause we faint not; but though our outward man perish, yet the inward *man* is renewed day by day.

### *Ephesians 2:1*

And you *hath he quickened*, who were dead in trespasses and sins;

## The Wayward Will

The 'shall' of God is mighty, certain,
voice of life beyond death's curtain,
Moses knew Jehovah's will
but struggled to align his will.

The 'shall' of God from Genesis
explains the will and was and is,
yet even though we know in head
we daily do not look ahead.

The 'shall' of God—a soaring tower
rendering puny human power,
Moses various trials passed
all for a season, none would last.

The 'shall' of God our faith sustains
for pharaohs ever bring us pains,
we'll fear nor trust no earthly sword
but bow before 'I *am* the LORD'.

# Exodus 7

BY THE TIME WE get to Exodus 7 Moses and Aaron are fully tuned instruments in the hand of Almighty God. Gone is that vacillating and prevaricating spirit, that self-doubt and equivocation. Present is that calm, obedient spirit that the Lord in His long-suffering and gentleness had spent decades bringing to fruition: "And Moses and Aaron went in unto Pharaoh, and they did so as the LORD had commanded . . ." (Exod 7:10). Just as Aaron would "cast down his rod" (v. 10), the Lord had set down Moses and Aaron as His chosen deliverers of Israel. Glory cannot be attributed to God's servants for it would then undercut the notion of their *being* servants. Equally, God's servants are most content and fulfilled when their Lord is, speaking reverently, in the driver's seat.

When things appear to be going wrong ("now the magicians of Egypt, they also did in like manner with their enchantments" v. 11), there is not a hint of grumbling or faltering in the faith of Moses or Aaron. Consequently, "Aaron's rod swallowed up their rods" (v. 12). When we trust in God's ways and submit to His thoughts, our ways and our thoughts become secondary to His: "Where *is* the wise? where *is* the scribe? where *is* the disputer of this world? hath not God made foolish the wisdom of this world?" (1 Cor 1:20). Our authority becomes higher than it ever could have been if we were left to our own devices; we are left "astonished" at what is being spoken and manifested through us as we submit to the One who "taught them as *one* having authority, and not as the scribes" (Matt 7:28, 29).

So close is the bond now that the Lord views Aaron's rod as "His" rod, the human instrument now working in alignment with Himself: "Thus saith the LORD, In this thou shalt know that I *am* the LORD: behold, I will smite with the rod that *is* in mine hand upon the waters which *are* in the river, and they shall be turned to blood" (v. 17). A few verses later it is hard to discern who exactly is doing the lifting; Moses, Aaron, or the Lord: "And

Moses and Aaron did so, as the LORD commanded; and he lifted up the rod" (v. 20). In a way it doesn't matter, for Christians are one in Christ and Christ is all that we know of God: "That they all may be one; as thou, Father, *art* in me, and I in thee, that they also may be one in us: that the world may believe that thou hast sent me" (John 17:21).

The pitiful digging of water holes around the revered and worshipped Nile river ("And all the Egyptians digged round about the river for water to drink" v. 24) shows the extent to which the world will go to avoid accepting God's will. There seem to be no lengths to which we will not go in order to avoid the price that sin demands—our very life-blood, our immortal souls. To those who have not been granted ears to hear and eyes to see, the message of salvation in Christ alone and not of any human merit reeks in our proud nostrils as "the savour of death unto death" (2 Cor 2:16). How much Pharaoh and the Egyptians represent *us* in our fallen, Adamic nature. Nothing less than a miracle in the soul can bring about that sense of heroic mission and counter-cultural departure embodied by Moses and Aaron, God's called servants.

As Moses a few chapters earlier seemed such an unlikely champion, maybe you are but a few life chapters away from God using you in a most extraordinary and unexpected way.

## VERSES UPON WHICH TO MEDITATE

*(ideally in each chapter's context)*

### *Matthew 7:28-29*

And it came to pass, when Jesus had ended these sayings, the people were astonished at his doctrine:

For he taught them as *one* having authority, and not as the scribes.

### *John 17:21*

That they all may be one; as thou, Father, *art* in me, and I in thee, that they also may be one in us: that the world may believe that thou hast sent me.

### *1 Corinthians 1:20*

Where *is* the wise? where *is* the scribe? where *is* the disputer of this world? hath not God made foolish the wisdom of this world?

### *2 Corinthians 2:16*

To the one *we are* the savour of death unto death; and to the other the savour of life unto life. And who is sufficient for these things?

## The Rod That Is in Mine Hand

As Aaron's rod devoured their serpents
Pharaoh's heart despised God's servants,
sons of Satan hate to see
that power, that call, ability.

As Aaron's rod made waters blood
proud Pharaoh's heart was boiling blood,
his own magicians mimicking
he stayed enthroned, DIY king.

As Aaron's rod was of the Lord
its price this world could not afford,
the Bible too was made, Amen
those humans Holy Spirit's pen.

As Aaron's rod brought life to death
the Lord withheld from fish their breath,
He withheld not His blood from us
who dead were, now breathe in Jesus.

# Exodus 8

THE INTRANSIGENCE OF BOTH Moses and Pharaoh is quite something. They each wholeheartedly stand for their respective kingdoms. Pharaoh's kingdom represents the arrogant trappings of commercial and geo-political greatness; Moses' kingdom the uncompromising purity and worship of the living God, and yet both men are utterly convinced that they are right and that each other's kingdom is an abomination.

Such is the case today, with the most resolute atheist as immovable in atheistic defiance as the godly pastor is in belief in the Bible, although with one difference; the man of God is unwilling to be deceitful, resort to diplomacy, or adopt any form of charm offensive, for he believes the devil can come even as an "angel of light" (2 Cor 11:14) and was perhaps the most alluring of all creatures ever created: "Thine heart was lifted up because of thy beauty, thou hast corrupted thy wisdom by reason of thy brightness" (Ezek 28:17).

Another thing which is worth noting is the *extent* of Moses desire for devotional purity. It is not enough for him to accept worship on any old terms; even to be permitted to worship God but in a corrupted, worldly manner is regarded by him as "abomination" (Exod 8:26). We have perhaps lost this habit of using strong language to describe heinous departures from God's word, but no less is it true in our day. For a church to replace a pulpit with a stage, to share a Bible with an electric guitar and rock drum-kit, is not merely unfortunate, immature, or worldly Christianity; it is in God's eyes "abomination". Moses and every godly pastor can have nothing to do with such things. Thus Moses *declares* God's will rather than dallying in diplomacy or debate: "We will go three days' journey into the wilderness, and sacrifice to the LORD our God, as he shall command us" (v. 27). Pharaoh agrees in principle but deceitfully denies the specifics, the three days: "And Pharaoh said, I will let you go, that ye may sacrifice to the LORD your God in the wilderness; only ye shall not go very far away: entreat for me" (v.28). There is the added insult of Pharaoh disingenuously pretending to enter into the spirit of true religion ("entreat for me").

Moses wastes no time in debating with Pharaoh, just as any faithful pastor ought not become ensnared by the traps of sneering atheists and hateful proponents, at least not in any formal, debating context, the pastor's call being to feed the hungry flock of believers and proclaim the Gospel to the world rather than debate the existence of God with a corrupt elite. Pharaoh's true colors emerge after the mercy of God has been manifested: "And Pharaoh hardened his heart at this time also, neither would he let the people go" (v.32). The world will never be satisfied with any amount of blessing the Lord in His mercy deems fit to bestow; it thinks itself hard done by, and for every 99.9% of blessings it bitterly blames God for the 0.1% that appears to go wrong. The fact that it has no sensitivity to God and is blind to "the signs of the times" (Matt 16:3) is due to its foundational philosophies being wrong, built on "sand" rather than "rock" (Matt 7:24–27).

If any reader is sitting on the fence then now is the time to get off. Linger not among the pyramids of abomination but flee as far as possible; three days' prayerful journey, mental or other, in order to worship God Almighty "in spirit and in truth" (John 4:24).

## Departures

# VERSES UPON WHICH TO MEDITATE

*(ideally in each chapter's context)*

### *Ezekiel 28:17*

Thine heart was lifted up because of thy beauty, thou hast corrupted thy wisdom by reason of thy brightness: I will cast thee to the ground, I will lay thee before kings, that they may behold thee.

### *Matthew 7:24-27*

Therefore whosoever heareth these sayings of mine, and doeth them, I will liken him unto a wise man, which built his house upon a rock:

And the rain descended, and the floods came, and the winds blew, and beat upon that house; and it fell not: for it was founded upon a rock.

And every one that heareth these sayings of mine, and doeth them not, shall be likened unto a foolish man, which built his house upon the sand:

And the rain descended, and the floods came, and the winds blew, and beat upon that house; and it fell: and great was the fall of it.

### *16:3*

And in the morning, *It will be* foul weather to day: for the sky is red and lowring. O *ye* hypocrites, ye can discern the face of the sky; but can ye not *discern* the signs of the times?

### *John 4:24*

God *is* a Spirit: and they that worship him must worship *him* in spirit and in truth.

### *2 Corinthians 11:14*

And no marvel; for Satan himself is transformed into an angel of light.

## The Abomination of the Egyptians

The flies and lice and frogs became
a curse magicians couldn't tame,
for woe betide this rebel king
who would not know creation's King.

For thus the frogs piled up and stank
just like his heart which would not thank,
God's mercy gave him pause to fight
pride welling up within respite.

The dust of earth was turned to lice
this man had turned his heart to ice,
magicians, powerless, could but linger
seeing in it God's own finger.

Swarms of insects did come next
his heart betrayed by body, vexed,
Pharaoh accepted Moses' zeal
kind words—false face—the devil's deal.

# Exodus 9

THE UNIVERSAL CHURCH OF Jesus Christ cuts across all times, cultures, and institutions. Yes we are to join ourselves to a local, Bible believing congregation but no, this is no guarantee of salvation and is but an outward manifestation of what is known to God alone, indicated by that solemn, awful picture of final judgement the Lord places before us in Matthew 25:31–33: "When the Son of man shall come in his glory, and all the holy angels with him, then shall he sit upon the throne of his glory: and before him shall be gathered all nations: and he shall separate them one from another, as a shepherd divideth *his* sheep from the goats: and he shall set the sheep on his right hand, but the goats on the left."

There will undoubtedly be a significant number of secret believers revealed at the end, like Nicodemus and Joseph of Arimathea; those who could either find no godly congregation or who for some other reason, eg. a severely melancholic temperament, physical disability, complicated necessities of work, threats of imminent torture and death, could not make it to the local religious services which regularly occurred whilst they lived on earth. So it was in Moses' time. Exodus 9 seems to suggest there were not a few souls, Israelite or other, who feared and obeyed God's word ("He that feared the word of the LORD among the servants of Pharaoh made his servants and his cattle flee into the houses" v.20).

Equally, we know from later chapters that there were many Israelites who murmured, disobeyed, and ended up perishing in the false worship of the "molten calf" (Exod 32). The Lord Jesus it is whom we need more than we need our next meal or religious meeting. He it is to whom we must cling, for this whole world will dissolve in a scenario worse than any temporal judgment of hail and fire, foretold in Matthew 24:12–14: "And because iniquity shall abound, the love of many shall wax cold. But he that shall endure unto the end, the same shall be saved. And this gospel of the kingdom shall be preached in all the world for a witness unto all nations; and then shall the end come."

Moses, meanwhile, demonstrates that sense of meekness and instrumentality to which all Christians should aspire. It is our highest duty and calling in life to *serve* God, not call attention to ourselves in the world's way of self-aggrandizement. When one thinks about it we know remarkably little about the personal details of a Moses or indeed a Paul or a John. Such saints would undoubtedly abhor any intention of ours to indulge in a form of fleshly hagiography. They would assuredly see themselves as not one whit above the lowliest of believers, from the thief at the cross to the elderly soul of our times who is saved in the dying embers of earthly existence. May we not be found looking unto a human instrument, but rather be being used instrumentally by the One who gave us the ability and desire to even contemplate approaching Him.

## VERSES UPON WHICH TO MEDITATE

*(ideally in each chapter's context)*

### *Matthew 24:12–14*

And because iniquity shall abound, the love of many shall wax cold.

But he that shall endure unto the end, the same shall be saved.

And this gospel of the kingdom shall be preached in all the world for a witness unto all nations; and then shall the end come.

### *25:31–33*

When the Son of man shall come in his glory, and all the holy angels with him, then shall he sit upon the throne of his glory:

And before him shall be gathered all nations: and he shall separate them one from another, as a shepherd divideth *his* sheep from the goats:

And he shall set the sheep on his right hand, but the goats on the left.

**Let My People Go**

Not all who dwell within the world
belong unto the world,
so all who claim they're Israel
are not all Israel.

Some servants of the wicked one
in private feared God's Son,
while most in Goshen saved from hail
would go so far yet fail.

Pharaoh was man, no 'god' unique
for God to all doth speak,
in chapters, blessings, life events
hearts choose hardness, not sense.

Each decade brings more sickness to
our dying frames death due,
magicians, lusts, possessions burn
right sheep, left goats, all turn.

# Exodus 10

THE SENSE OF URGENCY and impatience is palpable in this chapter, reminding us again of the fact that spiritually blind world leaders are all too often mere tools in the devil's hand: "the devil is come down unto you, having great wrath, because he knoweth that he hath but a short time" (Rev 12:12). This is of heightened relevance Anno Domini than it was Before Christ, due to the Lord Jesus Christ's death-blow dealt to the devil whilst victoriously enduring the Cross.

Sin is a progressively crippling disease; the plague of locusts bad enough yet yielding only a partial darkness: "so that the land was darkened" (Exod 10:15), not as potent as the ensuing darkness that would come by God's decree: "even darkness *which* may be felt" (v.21), "a thick darkness" (v.22). In our unregenerate condition we fail to interpret the events of geopolitical, national, and personal news aright, so are doomed to experience ever worsening judgment as time goes on. Our clenched hearts would have it so; we willfully bring it on ourselves.

A believer is one who no longer subscribes to the law of a clenched fist, one whose heart has been broken: "The sacrifices of God *are* a broken spirit: a broken and a contrite heart, O God, thou wilt not despise" (Ps 51:17). God's people know the worst about themselves, ergo seek the best not in themselves but in the One to whom they reverently give "sacrifices and burnt offerings" (Exod 10:25). There is nothing inherently different or better in a believer than in an unbeliever; however, a new nature, a foreign principle of righteousness comes into a soul and so that soul now sings to a different tune, one which to the worldly mind makes no sense and is abhorred.

Pharaoh's attempts at repentance and faith lack sincerity and are the vain babblings of a Machiavellian actor: "Now therefore forgive, I pray thee, my sin only this once, and intreat the LORD your God, that he may take away from me this death only" (v.17). The fact that he saw sin only as an isolated act with a limited consequence was evidence that, at root, he wasn't inclined to see himself as a hopeless sinner. Thus, he could not belong to the heavenly kingdom of our Lord Jesus Christ for the entry requirement is a complete not a partial cleansing, on His terms not ours: "If I wash thee not, thou hast no part with me" (John 13:8). A believer is one who has come to the end of self and is now living through Christ, unwilling to claim any righteousness outside of Him; not even "an hoof" of creaturely power and glory "left behind" (Exod 10:26), but all brought unto the King of heaven and earth, to be disposed of at He wills.

## VERSES UPON WHICH TO MEDITATE

*(ideally in each chapter's context)*

### *Psalm 51:17*

The sacrifices of God *are* a broken spirit: a broken and a contrite heart, O God, thou wilt not despise.

### *John 13:8*

Peter saith unto him, Thou shalt never wash my feet. Jesus answered him, If I wash thee not, thou hast no part with me.

### *Revelation 12:12*

Therefore rejoice, *ye* heavens, and ye that dwell in them. Woe to the inhabiters of the earth and of the sea! for the devil is come down unto you, having great wrath, because he knoweth that he hath but a short time.

## A Thick Darkness

As Adams build a ruined kingdom
saints from union must secede,
as Pharaoh raged against God's kingdom
servants warned of Egypt's plight.

As Adams make their false repentance
saints even of prayers repent,
as Pharaoh sought a stay of sentence
greater darkness soon would come.

As Adams always compromise
saints' lives will always sacrifice,
see Pharaoh battling for his prize
his war spectacularly lost.

As Adams ever God resist
saints love to dwell upon the LORD,
proud Pharaoh, life's whole point had missed
in hell forever finding face.

# Exodus 11

THIS CHAPTER WORKS ACCEPTABLY using the traditional historical-grammatical method; yet in the deeper spiritualizing principle of Galatians 4 ("Which things are an allegory" v.24), we may see Pharaoh and Moses as types of the "natural body" vs. "spiritual body", or "first man Adam" vs. "last Adam" respectively (1 Cor 15:44–45). Pharaoh in this sense represents the highest achievements that flesh can muster in its fallen condition; wealth, power, influence, control, yet "earthy" (v.47) ergo unable to "inherit the kingdom of God" (v.50). For the "image of the heavenly" to emerge (v.49) or rather be "born again", the reign of fallen man must end; in a legalistic, positional sense, every person needs first to have died before being raised up again, this time in Christ.

As with all types, though, there are limitations and generalizations. Sadly the jewels mentioned in verse 2 would be used for corrupted purposes not so very many chapters hence (Exod 32). "First man Adam" in this sense isn't fully purged at conversion but throughout the pilgrim life of sanctification needs progressively to be put to death every step of the way: "Mortify therefore your members which are upon the earth" (Col 3:5). In fact, the global reach of the gospel means that there will be "a great multitude, which no man could number, of all nations, and kindreds, and people, and tongues" (Rev 7:9). Israel—typical nation—would only be fulfilled in the truer *ecclesiastical* reality of the international church millennia later.

When an unregenerate soul, Israelite or Egyptian, is personally sought out and saved by the work of the Holy Spirit within, all tribal, ethnic, and nationalistic strains of pride are left behind, "for ye are all one in Christ Jesus" (Gal 3:28). This chapter points us to the promised land of Canaan yet also to the far greater glory of "Jerusalem which is above . . . which is the mother of us all" (Gal 4:26). Millenia later, we are still subject to death even in our blessed New Testament age; the same death that made Jesus weep, and yet a death which will one day be removed: "then shall be brought to pass the saying that is written, Death is swallowed up in victory" (1 Cor 15:54).

Meanwhile, as with "Moses and Aaron" when they "did all these wonders before Pharaoh: and the LORD hardened Pharaoh's heart, so that he would not let the children of Israel go out of his land" (Exod 11:10), we too are still being harried and harassed by one pharaoh after another; types of Satan, defeated yet persistent in opposing all things that are beloved of God. Satanic *Pharaoh* is one whose cruel kingdom willfully worships the rebellious fallen flesh, and whose deserved destiny is to be "tormented day and night for ever and ever" (Rev 20:10) with all those who would, if they could, permanently destroy the One who gave them life.

DEPARTURES

## VERSES UPON WHICH TO MEDITATE

*(ideally in each chapter's context)*

### *1 Corinthians 15:44-45, 47, 49-50, 54*

It is sown a natural body; it is raised a spiritual body. There is a natural body, and there is a spiritual body.

And so it is written, The first man Adam was *made* a living soul; the last Adam was made a quickening spirit.

The first man is of the earth, earthy: the second man is the Lord from heaven.

And as we have borne the image of the earthy, we shall also bear the image of the heavenly.

Now this I say, brethren, that flesh and blood cannot inherit the kingdom of God; neither doth corruption inherit incorruption.

So when this corruptible shall have put on incorruption, and this mortal shall have put on immortality, then shall be brought to pass the saying that is written, Death is swallowed up in victory.

### *Galatians 3:28*

There is neither Jew nor Greek, there is neither bond nor free, there is neither male nor female: for ye are all one in Christ Jesus.

### *4:24, 26*

Which things are an allegory: for these are the two covenants; the one from the mount Sinai, which gendereth to bondage, which is Agar.

But Jerusalem which is above is free, which is the mother of us all.

## Colossians 3:5

Mortify therefore your members which are upon the earth; fornication, uncleanness, inordinate affection, evil concupiscence, and covetousness, which is idolatry:

## Revelation 7:9

After this I beheld, and, lo, a great multitude, which no man could number, of all nations, and kindreds, and people, and tongues, stood before the throne, and before the Lamb, clothed with white robes, and palms in their hands;

### 20:10

And the devil that deceived them was cast into the lake of fire and brimstone, where the beast and the false prophet are, and shall be tormented day and night for ever and ever.

## The LORD Doth Put a Difference

And now the judgement day—behold
one final plague—firstborn to die,
to bring to birth new man from old
God's wonders to be multiplied.

The depth of sinful human heart
no end to rebels' hateful pride,
'twas time for Israel to depart
from earthy Egypt, God defied.

All jewels of silver, jewels of gold
bestowed by God as gifts unearned,
wage earners of the Sphinx's mould
to judgement bound, man-made, man-earned.

Salvation, all of God, not part
He will not share with creature, man,
as Christ-transformèd souls we start
to be in Him what He began.

# Exodus 12

In light of Augustine's 'the Old Testament is the New concealed, the New Testament the Old revealed', an allegorical, Christ-centric exegesis of this first Passover in Exodus 12 seems right and proper (as in 1 Cor 10:11, Rom 15:4), for I am reminded that "the precious blood of Christ was foreordained before the foundation of the world" (1 Pet 1:19–20) and that He is "the Lamb slain from the foundation of the world" (Rev 13:8). How much greater the antitype than the type as our hearts bow, knowing that our sin-natures are done away with, our sin-mountains 'passed over'.

His arms are outstretched towards the world but we will not come. Some in time are secretly inclined towards Him as the Holy Spirit sovereignly works. Others are left to work out their own damnation as they willfully and consistently reject Him, despite the numerous crossroads at which they could have turned with tender supplications and cryings out if they would. It all boils down to one Man and one night; in fact, a day in which the very creation lowered its veil as if the awfulness and unspeakableness of the God-man's sufferings could not be viewed. Who can conceive of Him experiencing the everlasting punishment of billions in the span of a few created hours? Such things are not to be comprehended but perceived, as we receive the gift of repentance, faith, and the Spirit within.

Foreigners to faith, strangers to repentance, all are invited. Citizens from deeply pagan, atheistic cultures are welcomed. Sinners of high degree and low degree, relative wickedness and abominable wickedness are bidden. Men, women, and children who dwell in comparative civilization and so-called savagery are all equally called to come to "the Lamb of God, which taketh away the sin of the world" (John 1:29). There is no one who cannot come and find forgiveness through Him; equally, there is no one who can stand on their own two feet without Him, no one who can plead ignorance, claim self-righteousness, blame a poor upbringing, a godless education, social pressure, or governmental indoctrination.

All souls will come, either horror-stricken to the "great white throne" of judgement (Rev 20:11) or laden with joy within the soul-saving "first resurrection" (v.6). With God there are no excuses, no favorites who can escape the just punishment of His perfect moral law. There is not a soul in heaven who trusted *not* in the substitutionary atonement of the Lamb whilst walking and talking in physical and mental health on earth. What an emptiness and a mockery it is when we dwell comfortably with those who turn so-called Easter into a time of bunnies, eggs, and rituals, when all around us are dying men to whom we should be preaching with all earnestness and personal inadequacy "Jesus Christ, and him crucified" (1 Cor 2:2) so "that no flesh should glory in his presence" (1:29).

May it be that with you and your house that there will be "a great cry" (Exod 12:30) not of eternal loss, but of joy in the Lord as you contemplate this incarnate—crucified—risen—reigning Monarch, not in His Christmas card depictions but in His awesome glory to redeem and His terrifying power to damn.

# Exodus 12

## VERSES UPON WHICH TO MEDITATE

*(ideally in each chapter's context)*

### John 1:29

The next day John seeth Jesus coming unto him, and saith, Behold the Lamb of God, which taketh away the sin of the world.

### Romans 15:4

For whatsoever things were written aforetime were written for our learning, that we through patience and comfort of the scriptures might have hope.

### 1 Corinthians 1:19, 29

For it is written, I will destroy the wisdom of the wise, and will bring to nothing the understanding of the prudent.

That no flesh should glory in his presence.

### 2:2

For I determined not to know any thing among you, save Jesus Christ, and him crucified.

### 10:11

Now all these things happened unto them for ensamples: and they are written for our admonition, upon whom the ends of the world are come.

### *1 Peter 1:19-20*

But with the precious blood of Christ, as of a lamb without blemish and without spot:

Who verily was foreordained before the foundation of the world, but was manifest in these last times for you,

### **Revelation 13:8**

And all that dwell upon the earth shall worship him, whose names are not written in the book of life of the Lamb slain from the foundation of the world.

### *20:6, 11*

Blessed and holy *is* he that hath part in the first resurrection: on such the second death hath no power, but they shall be priests of God and of Christ, and shall reign with him a thousand years.

And I saw a great white throne, and him that sat on it, from whose face the earth and the heaven fled away; and there was found no place for them.

**That Night of the LORD**

The holy killing of the lamb,
the blood by faith on each door jamb,
the shunning of the leavened bread
pride mortified, now left for dead.

The Lamb of God thus signified
unblemished Adam crucified,
wine-blood, bread-body, all a token
Jesus' body, for us broken.

Foreigners and strangers all
beneath the shadow of the Fall,
each heart must circumcisèd be
only the born again go free.

Pass over, Lord, my waywardness
see me in alien righteousness,
purge me so fruit of Christ may grow
live me, daily I die below.

# Exodus 13

IT TOOK A MIGHTY and direct miracle to bring those few million, literal Israelites out of the land of bondage: "for by strength of hand the LORD brought you out from this *place*" (v.3), just as a soul brought out of darkness into Christ is living, breathing evidence of what God will bring about for His glory. Indeed, scores of generations to come were in the divine mind, the elemental picture language of animals, bread, blood, cloud, and fire being employed, just as the Christian delights and rejoices in being saved once and for all by Christ, and then has a lifetime in which to "work out" one's "own salvation by fear and trembling" (Phil 2:12).

The traditionally called Lord's prayer teaches us that the majority of believers on earth are left here so that God's "will be done in earth, as *it is* in heaven" (Matt 6:10). To live on earth for the duration of decades is not to waste time but to enjoy the privilege of "redeeming the time" (Eph 5:16), for even on earth "to live *is* Christ" (Phil 1:21). Were it instead God's will simply to reprieve and redeem us all as thieves on the cross in the final minutes before execution, then the gradual and methodical unfolding of instructive, God-breathed Scripture would have been, dare I say, superfluous.

God knows what we have been designed to give, and when we can endure certain preordained challenges and trials. To have plunged this fledgling theocratic nation into "the way of the land of the Philistines" (Exod 13:17) too soon may have been to destroy its new-found courage and strength. To have prematurely withdrawn the immediacy and Fatherly provision of the "pillar of a cloud" and "pillar of fire" (v. 21) may have been akin to planting a newly 'born again' believer into the pulpit or mission field, green and unseasoned.

God's strength is eternal, unchangeable, and inexhaustible. Believers' strength waxes and wanes, growing incrementally, sometimes painfully slowly, over a series of sanctified tests in which we may fall "seven times" but by faith rise "up again" (Prov 24:16). Persistent unbelievers, by contrast, are those who sin by nature and inclination, lacking the grace to seek anything outside of an imagined self-righteousness: "there shall be no reward to the evil *man*; the candle of the wicked shall be put out" (v. 20).

Let us not rest merely in religion, then, for it is in Christ that we have what we continually need. It behooves us to remember how the vast majority of Moses' adult contemporaries perished under judgement: "So I sware in my wrath, They shall not enter into my rest" (Heb 3:11). God forbid that we should allegorize and spiritualize Scripture to the extent that we regard these real people only as theoretical types of besetting sins, rather than as very real warnings *about* real people *for* real people Anno Domini, who may have started out well, only to end up "having damnation, because they have cast off their first faith" (1 Tim 5:12).

Departures

## VERSES UPON WHICH TO MEDITATE

*(ideally in each chapter's context)*

### *Proverbs 24:16, 20*

For a just man falleth seven times, and riseth up again: but the wicked shall fall into mischief.

For there shall be no reward to the evil *man*; the candle of the wicked shall be put out.

### *Matthew 6:10*

Thy kingdom come. Thy will be done in earth, as *it is* in heaven.

### *Ephesians 5:16*

Redeeming the time, because the days are evil.

### *Philippians 1:21*

For to me to live *is* Christ, and to die *is* gain.

### *2:12*

Wherefore, my beloved, as ye have always obeyed, not as in my presence only, but now much more in my absence, work out your own salvation with fear and trembling.

### *1 Timothy 5:12*

Having damnation, because they have cast off their first faith.

### *Hebrews 3:11*

So I sware in my wrath, They shall not enter into my rest.)

## And the LORD Went before Them

That pillar cloud, our precious Book,
so full of heaven's mystery,
that fiery pillar, holy fury
map redeeming history.

Those Philistines, idolaters
vengeful, warlike, forever restless,
sins besetting, upset us
new faith can sometimes lapse, listless.

Unleavened bread, blood substitute
such visual aids given to teach us,
Deity to human wed
our Bridegroom comes from far to reach us.

First man spurned God, self, and wife
firstborn hated, murdered his brother,
Firstborn from the Virgin's womb
releases us from self and other.

# Exodus 14

THE NOTION OF TAKING a sledgehammer to crack a nut comes to mind when we read of Pharaoh personally involving himself in the hunting down of the minority slave workers who had recently been troubling a part of his kingdom: "And he took six hundred chosen chariots, and all the chariots of Egypt" (Exod 14:7); six of course being symbolic of man's supposed power and glory, seven of God's perfection. As in more modern history with the likes of Hitler or Stalin, all their tanks, nuclear rockets, and space programs are a) designed ultimately as weapons of war against God, and b) doomed to failure because of this, hence why our attention is drawn away from any greatness inherent in a nation, and towards the certain hope that "the LORD shall fight for you, and ye shall hold your peace" (v.14).

The lesson for New Testament Christians is not to depend upon military might, political prowess, or anything else that might appeal to fallen flesh. If it were our Father's will for us to take on the devil's project by such means then we would be given "more than twelve legions of angels" (Matt 26:53) in order to put down every ungodly assault. Gone would be all forms of sexual perversion, abortion, atheism, Darwinism, sweatshops, and every other shameful abomination which darkens this doomed earth. Yes the kingdom of Christ "is not of this world" (John 18:36) and so we are not to fight to commandeer it, but rather implore souls to spiritually *depart* from its thinking, wholly trusting in "the angel of God" (Exod 14:19) or rather Jesus Christ and His holy, soul-saving rescue mission.

Human instrumentality is another lesson for us who live millenia on from these actual historical events recorded for us in Scripture. As in Exodus 14, so too the 'congregation' of today implores its 'under-shepherd' or pastor for help ("And they said to Moses" v. 11, "And Moses said unto the people" v. 13). All appointed servants of God, having no inherent power, prayerfully invoke the name of God ("The LORD shall fight for you" v. 14), passively receive His word ("And the LORD said unto Moses" v.15), and are filled with specific instructions to be executed by faith ("But lift thou up thy rod" v.16, "And Moses stretched out his hand" v.21), whilst placing all the credit and glory where it belongs, ie. with the Lord ("Thus the LORD saved Israel" v.30, "And Israel saw that great work which the LORD did" v.31).

We are warned in James 3:1 about the awful weight and responsibility of godly leadership which warrants a greater than usual standard of godly living, practical wisdom, and application of the now completed Scriptures: "My brethren, be not many masters, knowing that we shall receive the greater condemnation." We are about to approach the pinnacle of contentment in the earthly sojourn of those Israelites in the wilderness, in that most wonderful prayer of praise and thanksgiving (Exod 15). However, there will be murmuring (ch.16), discontentment (ch.17), exhaustion (ch.18), sanctified aloneness (ch.19—31), rank apostasy (ch.32), and demanding instructions (ch.32—40) ahead, such being the lot of those who would be pastors and deacons among the body of Christ on earth.

Nevertheless, we return to Exodus 14 and 15 which for Christians reflects that special time of consciously going from darkness into light, doubt into belief, uncertainty into assurance of forgiveness. The Lord deigns to see us not as we are in ourselves but as we are in Christ: "And the angel of God, which went before the camp of Israel, removed and went behind them; and the pillar of the cloud went from before their face, and stood behind them" (Exod 14:19). Solemnly He views this fallen, vindictive world not as it chooses to see itself but as it appears through the lens of Scripture: "And it came to pass, that in the morning watch the LORD looked unto the host of the Egyptians through the pillar of fire and of the cloud" (v.24).

If we are in Christ and daily in the Scriptures we have nothing to fear. If we are going our own way, seeking to drive our chariot wheels into the ever thickening mud then we are lost; not only lost, but irrevocably damned: "For Moses truly said unto the fathers, A prophet shall the Lord your God raise up unto you of your brethren, like unto me; him shall ye hear in all things whatsoever he shall say unto you. And it shall come to pass, *that* every soul, which will not hear that prophet, shall be destroyed from among the people" (Acts 3:22–23).

## VERSES UPON WHICH TO MEDITATE

*(ideally in each chapter's context)*

### Matthew 26:53

Thinkest thou that I cannot now pray to my Father, and he shall presently give me more than twelve legions of angels?

### John 18:36

Jesus answered, My kingdom is not of this world: if my kingdom were of this world, then would my servants fight, that I should not be delivered to the Jews: but now is my kingdom not from hence.

### Acts 3:22–23

For Moses truly said unto the fathers, A prophet shall the Lord your God raise up unto you of your brethren, like unto me; him shall ye hear in all things whatsoever he shall say unto you.

And it shall come to pass, *that* every soul, which will not hear that prophet, shall be destroyed from among the people.

### James 3:1

My brethren, be not many masters, knowing that we shall receive the greater condemnation.

## Thus the LORD Saved Israel

The world believers view entangled
slavish, not as stars bespangled,
futile, trapped in wilderness
remarkable in uselessness.

Yet Pharaoh could not leave alone,
inside him he could not disown,
he had to win the argument
his pride restore, his strength augment.

See Pharoah's roar, Moses' subside
surrounded now on every side,
man's chariots flash, saints wilt in grief
believers mourn their unbelief.

God's word is like a holy cloud
descending on a saint in crowd,
therein all panic fades away
Christ rose, He is the only way.

# Exodus 15

THIS WORSHIPFUL INTERRUPTION OF the redemptive narrative reveals the love of God in the heart of man, for who can restrain oneself when remembering the time of one's conversion, whether it was a day or a period of time. The language of possession seems outrageous and arrogant to the worldly or religiously minded: "my strength . . . my salvation . . . my God . . . my father's God" (v.2). How presumptuous, the worldly-religious might think, how deluded this makes the believer sound; and yet it is the inevitable consequence of the Holy Spirit taking up residence within a human, somewhat akin to romantic or parental love which similarly excludes and baffles those not included in its orbit. It is altogether on a different plane, though, and woe betide anyone who attempts to lower the Almighty to our level: "Who *is* like unto thee, O LORD, among the gods? who *is* like thee, glorious in holiness, fearful *in* praises, doing wonders?" (v.11).

It is all too easy to look back, since Moses and Israel have left such a significant imprint upon our Judeo-Christian civilization. It behooves us to remember that at this point in time they were a dispossessed people of perhaps a few million, without a Bible, situated in a desert hinterland, their future as yet unrevealed. It is all the more remarkable when Moses rejoices in "the mountain of thine inheritance . . . the Sanctuary" (v.17), assured of being in a place of absolute security. Such is the case with the 'born again' whose foundation has changed, whose hearts have been circumcised, their eyes opened to a new realm of spiritual reality hitherto unknown.

Rumblings of discontent enter in ominously when "the people murmured against Moses" (v.24). Deliverance from Pharaoh (tool of Satan) was sudden and breath-taking: "Thy right hand, O LORD, is become glorious in power: thy right hand, O LORD, hath dashed in pieces the enemy" (v. 6); but journeying to the promised land is a more gradual process through which souls must learn to live by faith, putting their trust in God's provision and promises revealed to them through God's under-shepherd, in this case Moses. Our heavenward pilgrimage is a gradual and seemingly slow sanctification that allows us to "prove" (Gal 6:4) the relative growth and authenticity of our faith by mirroring our lives against God's never-changing moral law: "if thou wilt diligently hearken . . . and wilt give ear . . . and keep . . ." (v.26) which we can do only through Christ.

All along life's pathway is the tree of Calvary upon which we may meditate and return; that which makes all bitterness palatable and pleasant: "And at midnight Paul and Silas prayed, and sang praises unto God" (Acts 16:25). The One who conquered death upon the "tree" (Gal 3:13) to undo the curse of our taking from the "tree" (Gen 3:6) is with us, whether we are in a relatively pleasant airy office in the middle of a metropolis, or in a boiling hot cramped punishment container in the middle of nowhere. When we look to Christ the troubling waters of life's unfolding providences are indeed made sweet (Exod 15:25), and along with Moses, Miriam, Paul, and Silas we sing His praises with as much gusto as our feeble frames can muster.

## VERSES UPON WHICH TO MEDITATE

*(ideally in each chapter's context)*

### *Genesis 3:6*

And when the woman saw that the tree *was* good for food, and that it *was* pleasant to the eyes, and a tree to be desired to make *one* wise, she took of the fruit thereof, and did eat, and gave also unto her husband with her; and he did eat.

### *Acts 16:25*

And at midnight Paul and Silas prayed, and sang praises unto God: and the prisoners heard them.

### *Galatians 3:13*

Christ hath redeemed us from the curse of the law, being made a curse for us: for it is written, Cursed *is* every one that hangeth on a tree:

### *6:4*

But let every man prove his own work, and then shall he have rejoicing in himself alone, and not in another.

## The LORD Is My Strength and Song

Man's joy in God must overspill
its magma sparks dance, flow and cool,
God did through Moses Pharaoh kill
one now seen wise, one now a fool.

No strength by Israel was claimed
the LORD performed what they could not,
God's mercy openly proclaimed
to human souls Egypt forgot.

The wilderness awaiting now
the holy life bitter at first,
God sanctifies and teaches how
believers are to hunger, thirst.

The tree a symbol of the Fall
also a glimpse of Calvary,
we're saved from sin, not partial—all,
to serve the Lord, increasingly.

# Exodus 16

THAT BLISSFUL PLACE OF conversion and justification (Elim) contains God's perfection, 12 ("twelve wells") and 70 ("three-score and ten"), Exodus 15:27 representing completion in terms of the elect who are to be saved from this world, and the finished, victorious 'cross-work' of our Lord Jesus Christ. Now, however, we are to continue on our pilgrimage to the ultimate promised land (heaven), *in* the world but "not of" it (John 17:16). There is, in the majority of cases, no short-cut for we all must receive daily provision, learning to "seek . . . first the kingdom of God, and his righteousness; and all these things shall be added unto" us (Matt 6:33).

We are travelling through this worldly "wilderness of Sin" by grace, yes, but Christian maturity must at some point confront the reality of the moral law ("Elim and Sinai" Exod 16:1). We love Jesus, yes, or rather depend upon His love for us: "As the Father hath loved me, so have I loved you: continue ye in my love" (John 15:9). However, we are to mature and grow in the faith and so increasingly be fulfilling God's moral law through Christ the way: "If ye keep my commandments, ye shall abide in my love; even as I have kept my Father's commandments, and abide in his love" (v.10).

All too often we are distracted by worldly problems such as job, house, education, possessions, and health. Yet we are being trained by our long-suffering, loving heavenly Father to rely upon His provision for our temporal needs, so that we may more perfectly meditate upon and worship Him, in this case by honoring His creation ordinance of a weekly day of rest: "See, for that the LORD hath given you the sabbath" (Exod 16:29). This gift is at first accepted almost reluctantly and with plenty of concerns within our too distracted minds, thus we may rest dutifully but without mention of abiding joy and heartfelt praise: "So the people rested on the seventh day" (v.30).

Increasingly, though, we feel inclined to develop a more consistent taste for God's word, which gradually grows to become more and more important in our lives. Our reading of the Bible, at first short and superficial "like wafers", comes to be enriched and deepened as we go along Christ's narrow way, our souls finding this strangely satisfying spiritual nourishment to be "with honey" (Exod 16:31) as we feast upon it throughout our earthly pilgrimage.

Whatever may happen to us, it is this "Manna" or spiritual Word of provision that sustains us and keeps us going. How else can we bear to dwell continually within this sin-sick, Christ-hating world in which even and especially our own indwelling sins appall us? How could martyrs be burned whilst singing hymns of praise to God, or missionaries willingly travel across this world to preach Christ and die young, were it not for the "honey" of God's word on lips, minds, hearts, deeply sanctifying the soul: "For which cause we faint not; but though our outward man perish, yet the inward *man* is renewed day by day. For our light affliction, which is but for a moment, worketh for us a far more exceeding *and* eternal weight of glory" (2 Cor 4:16–17). Thanks be to God.

## VERSES UPON WHICH TO MEDITATE

*(ideally in each chapter's context)*

### *Matthew 6:33*

But seek ye first the kingdom of God, and his righteousness; and all these things shall be added unto you.

### *John 15:9-10*

As the Father hath loved me, so have I loved you: continue ye in my love.

If ye keep my commandments, ye shall abide in my love; even as I have kept my Father's commandments, and abide in his love.

### *17:16*

They are not of the world, even as I am not of the world.

### *2 Corinthians 4:16-17*

For which cause we faint not; but though our outward man perish, yet the inward *man* is renewed day by day.

For our light affliction, which is but for a moment, worketh for us a far more exceeding *and* eternal weight of glory;

## The Children of Israel Murmured

From Elim every Christian goes
after the bliss of second birth,
unto this world the Christian shows
what faith is like, God's will on earth.

A part of you wants to return
to Egypt where the self did rule,
the other part for God does burn
His grace, deep in your soul, faith's fuel.

We learn to digest Holy word
at first the taste foreign and strange,
then teething comes, then sour mood
then tantrums, all in Father's range.

Provision made for every child
of God who truly rests in Him,
look on your days, your Father's mild,
deserving hell—rise, shine, don't dim.

# Exodus 17

IT BEHOOVES US TO compare this chapter with the seemingly similar passage in Numbers 20 in order to set it in its proper context and see what progress, if any, exists for our instruction. It seems that the account in Exodus occurred not long after the dramatic and powerful exodus from bondage in Egypt, while the account in Numbers occurred years later when Israel had been wending its way to the promised land for quite some time. We may see in both accounts, respectively, the "goodness and severity of God" (Rom 11:22) in which those Israelites of pilgrimage like us churched ones of New Testament times, should have known better, and so we are warned never to stop spiritually striving until we are truly home: "Wherefore let him that thinketh he standeth take heed lest he fall" (1 Cor 10:12).

God's goodness can be seen in this first Exodus account of the trial of faith surrounding that most life-giving of things—water. The Lord is long-suffering and understanding of His people's spiritual immaturity, impatience, and relative (but not absolute) faithlessness, through Moses going before them: "Behold, I will stand before thee", using Moses as a model of faith: "And Moses did so" (Exod 17:6), and as a type of Christ for the benefit of the "elders of Israel" (v.6) that they might learn to lean more fully on their ultimate Redeemer.

Exodus 17 thus presents us with the valuable lesson of prayerful struggle and an inward life of spiritual warfare which God has promised to honor and reward. Moses, after all, labored in prayer as we struggle in prayer, aided by his fellow believers: "But Moses' hands were heavy ... and Aaron and Hur stayed up his hands" (v.12). It points to the mighty battles that Joshua (another type of Christ) would face on his people's behalf. For the New Testament believer it points to the weekly prayer meeting as a thing of highest priority; what blessings we forfeit when do not attend it.

God's goodness is seen in that, despite nearly a whole adult generation of Israelites perishing through unbelief ("your fathers tempted me... forty years... not known my ways... not enter into my rest" Heb 3:9–11), Israel as a whole *would* enter in, as seen in the Book of Joshua. So there is a warfare to be waged within the heart of every believer, justification by Christ leading to sanctification through Christ.

Moreover, the believer's outward battles are with this world, blinded and led as it is by Satan (2 Cor 4:4), utterly inimical to all that God loves and represents of Himself in this sin-sick, benighted global culture. We have the promise that this world's culture, represented in this chapter by Amalek, will be "utterly put out" of "remembrance" (Exod 17:14), and that until that time "the LORD *will have* war with Amalek from generation to generation" (v.16).

It may seem to us that in our day the cause of Christ is lost, especially in the secular, highly influential, arrogant West. However, we are to hold up "Jehovah-nissi" (v.15)—the LORD my banner, through Moses' example of zealous prayer and spiritual edification. Our Bibles should regularly be in our hands, our thoughts regularly turning to prayer and meditation, that we might be like the vigilant "goodman of the house" (Matt 24:43), overjoyed rather than dismayed when the Omega suddenly and gloriously returns.

The parallel passage, years later in Numbers, shows us that while God's "goodness" is real, so too is His "severity". These more spiritually exercised Israelites of later years provoked Moses to:

- ungodly anger: "Hear now, ye rebels; must we fetch you water out of this rock?" (Num 20:10), "they angered him" (Ps 106:32), "he spake unadvisedly with his lips" (v. 33),
- ungodly over-reaching: "he smote the rock twice" (Num 20:11), "so that it went ill with Moses for their sakes" (Ps 106:33)
- a less than sanctified treatment of what should have been a solemn, spiritual lesson: "ye believed me not, to sanctify me in the eyes of the children of Israel" (Num 20:12)
- mar the spiritual edification of God's people: "spiritual drink... spiritual Rock... Christ" (1 Cor 10:4).

For Israel it was not merely a question of anger, words, disobedience, or nourishment but at root a failure of love for and trust in God: "Because they believed not in God, and trusted not in his salvation" (Ps 78:22). As with the statistically acknowledged church of circa 2 billion souls in our present day, we know that the vast majority is not saved, neither knowing nor honoring the Word of God or the God of the Word; hell awaiting each soul unless each personally repents and believes *in* Jesus and believes Jesus. Nevertheless, through God's goodness and severity His perfect plan is being worked out on earth as it is in heaven, because He would indeed be "sanctified in them" (Num 20:13) as He will be sanctified in us who believe. The rebellion and unbelief of our race can in no way thwart the Almighty will of our Sovereign God, no matter how hard it tries.

# Exodus 17

## VERSES UPON WHICH TO MEDITATE

*(ideally in each chapter's context)*

### Numbers 20:10-13

And Moses and Aaron gathered the congregation together before the rock, and he said unto them, Hear now, ye rebels; must we fetch you water out of this rock?

And Moses lifted up his hand, and with his rod he smote the rock twice: and the water came out abundantly, and the congregation drank, and their beasts also.

And the LORD spake unto Moses and Aaron, Because ye believed me not, to sanctify me in the eyes of the children of Israel, therefore ye shall not bring this congregation into the land which I have given them.

This *is* the water of Meribah; because the children of Israel strove with the LORD, and he was sanctified in them.

### Psalm 78:22

Because they believed not in God, and trusted not in his salvation:

### 106:32-33

They angered *him* also at the waters of strife, so that it went ill with Moses for their sakes:

Because they provoked his spirit, so that he spake unadvisedly with his lips.

### Matthew 24:43

But know this, that if the goodman of the house had known in what watch the thief would come, he would have watched, and would not have suffered his house to be broken up.

### *Romans 11:22*

Behold therefore the goodness and severity of God: on them which fell, severity; but toward thee, goodness, if thou continue in his goodness: otherwise thou also shalt be cut off.

### *1 Corinthians 10:4, 12*

And did all drink the same spiritual drink: for they drank of that spiritual Rock that followed them: and that Rock was Christ.

### *2 Corinthians 4:4*

In whom the god of this world hath blinded the minds of them which believe not, lest the light of the glorious gospel of Christ, who is the image of God, should shine unto them.

### *Hebrews 3:9-11*

When your fathers tempted me, proved me, and saw my works forty years.

Wherefore I was grieved with that generation, and said, They do alway err in *their* heart; and they have not known my ways.

So I sware in my wrath, They shall not enter into my rest.

## The Chiding of the Children of Israel

The Rock of Christ, smitten for us
the Source from whom live waters flow,
no soul who disbelieves God's 'Thus'
will ever into heaven go.

The best of men are men at best
the Rock was to be sanctified,
Moses, Israel, put to the test
all failed, and so the Savior died.

But Israel, failing, turned to prayer
by faith his rod was held aloft,
through human means God kept it there
through Hur, Aaron, not standing by.

And even here Christ typified,
the Son of Man, arms fixed, outstretched,
Jesus aloft, in Him we died
to rise again, lost sinners fetched.

# Exodus 18

WE HAVE HERE A beautiful type of Christ receiving His bride, the church (Zipporah), comprised of *justification* (Eliezer—"God . . . mine help . . . delivered me from the sword of Pharaoh" v.4) and *sanctification* (Gershom—"an alien in a strange land" v.3). Moses will later represent *glorification* ("the skin of his face shone" Exod 34:30), but for now the travails of wilderness journeying are very much in the foreground. Romans 8, by comparison, conflates these two doctrinal book-ends ("and whom he justified, them he also glorified" v. 30), having passed through the previous chapter of sanctification: "O wretched man that I am!" (7:24).

What impresses us deeply is Moses' willingness to listen, learn, and be instructed. What right had Jethro, he might have thought, to advise *him*—God's mighty Exodus superman of amazing deliverance. One can think of a hundred worldly examples throughout history in which the man of the moment would not listen to one iota of advice from anyone, let alone someone from another group not immediately connected with his group in the ascendancy. God's people will, therefore, humbly lean upon "all that the LORD had done" (Exod 18:8), *not* upon their own perceived prowess or greatness. They will also be amenable to God speaking to them through Scripture but also Providence, be it circumstantial or conversational. In God's goodness He has permitted wisdom to come through multiple sources; we are not hermetically sealed off from history and society, and there are times at which wisdom may come through a surprising source, such as a colleague at work or friend from another denominational persuasion.

Then there is the potential threat to Moses' ego: "thou art not able to perform it thyself alone" (Exod 18:18). These words are an abomination to the flesh which likes to be told the opposite, ie. you can do it all and you can do it all your*self*; precisely what Satan was stoking up in the Garden of Eden: "in the day ye eat thereof, then your eyes shall be opened, and ye shall be as gods" (Gen 3:5). The world is full of *self*—darling icons, celebrities, heroes, winners. The godly, by contrast, are seen as "base things of the world, and things which are despised" (1 Cor 1:28). However, the godly are honest, open, and willing to be "God-ward" so that they "mayest bring the causes unto God" (Exod 18:19). Only when coming to the end of self will the godly be of use to others.

The making of Moses, then, is humility; the realization of his own inability through an unexpected source, a humility which allowed him and allows us to "grow in grace, and *in* the knowledge of our Lord and Savior Jesus Christ" (2 Pet 3:18). His life would increasingly point to Christ, the "Prophet" of prophets who would finally, authoritatively bring about the fulfillment of all that was now in embryo; "like unto" Moses but infinitely greater: "unto him ye shall hearken" (Deut 18:15).

In fact, the words of John the Baptist uttered over a millennium later could very well have been spoken by Moses and are indeed echoed by every true pastor, deacon, elder, and believer under the sun: "He must increase, but I *must* decrease. He that cometh from above is above all: he that is of the earth is earthly, and speaketh of the earth: he that cometh from heaven is above all" (John 3:30–31).

## VERSES UPON WHICH TO MEDITATE

*(ideally in each chapter's context)*

### *Genesis 3:5*

For God doth know that in the day ye eat thereof, then your eyes shall be opened, and ye shall be as gods, knowing good and evil.

### *Exodus 34:30*

And when Aaron and all the children of Israel saw Moses, behold, the skin of his face shone; and they were afraid to come nigh him.

### *Deuteronomy 18:15*

The LORD thy God will raise up unto thee a Prophet from the midst of thee, of thy brethren, like unto me; unto him ye shall hearken;

### *John 3:30–31*

He must increase, but I *must* decrease.

He that cometh from above is above all: he that is of the earth is earthly, and speaketh of the earth: he that cometh from heaven is above all.

### *Romans 7:24*

O wretched man that I am! who shall deliver me from the body of this death?

### *8:30*

Moreover whom he did predestinate, them he also called: and whom he called, them he also justified: and whom he justified, them he also glorified.

## Exodus 18

### *1 Corinthians 1:28*

And base things of the world, and things which are despised, hath God chosen, *yea*, and things which are not, to bring to nought things that are:

### *2 Peter 3:18*

But grow in grace, and in the knowledge of our Lord and Saviour Jesus Christ. To him be glory both now and for ever. Amen.

## For This Thing Is Too Heavy for Thee

A blessèd picture, Zipporah,
renewing vows of holy love,
received by God's deliverer
a type of Christ, 'the Head' above.

'Eliezer', called once to depart
sin's pyramids, for 'justified',
'Gershom', God's people set apart
through wilderness, so 'sanctified'.

Another picture, Christ the judge
to whom each soul must give account,
so Moses sat and did not budge,
from dawn to dusk, each soul did count.

But Jethro saw it wouldn't work
for Moses solo couldn't cope,
while Jesus listens, millions lurk
He only reigns—the sinner's hope.

# Exodus 19

WE HAVE HERE THE superficially perplexing proposition of the "living God" as a terrifying presence, One into whose hands it is a "fearful thing to fall" (Heb 10:31). This, despite the "eagles' wings" (Exod 19:4) of deliverance from the dead. Why, we may ask, the fear and terror of being "put to death" (v.12) or "stoned, or shot through" (v.13) if even a hand were to touch the mountain reserved for Moses alone? Well, the answer is to be found as always in Christ, the divine antitype to so many Old Testament types. For if any of us even for an instant believes oneself able to stand in the presence of God *without* a mediator, then one is sadly deluded and in danger of not even having the basics of saving faith.

We live in a fallen world, one which is under the curse of death and everlasting judgement. Despite the blessings of nourishment and food revealed in previous chapters, this chapter brings us to the stark reality that we stand as beggars, cured lepers, gracious recipients of a holy God's sovereign favor, or we do not stand at all. The saved sinner knows that Christ has descended into the depths and risen to the heights for the soul's everlasting sake. Thus, it is spiritual madness and ingratitude to think for an instant of standing outside of Him, as it were "to bring Christ down *from above*" (Rom 10:6) or "to bring up Christ again from the dead" (v.7). He has done all that we could not do, and is the "one mediator between God and men, the man Christ Jesus" (1 Tim 2:5).

Thus, as the God-man warns of hell in His Sermon on the Mount, God's man (Moses) speaks God's words here, with the purpose of weaning the children of Israel off the 'milk' of mere deliverance from slavery (from this fallen world system) and on to spiritual maturity whereby it will actually fulfill its 'meaty' role as "a kingdom of priests, and an holy nation" (Exod 19:6), a beacon of hope to the people of other nations, realized more fully in a later time: "And there came of all people to hear the wisdom of

Solomon, from all kings of the earth, which had heard of his wisdom" (1 Kgs 4:34).

The believer's life post conversion is one of sanctification. As in chapter 18 it is this second pillar which defines the true *ekklesia*, the other being justification. To base a life of faith on only one of these two pillars results in an imbalanced and precarious pilgrimage. If these two are well balanced then all is well, and the crowning cornerstone of glorification will be apprehended: "And ye are Christ's; and Christ *is* God's" (1 Cor 3:23). We are commanded to revere and have the highest possible regard for God's ways, and in particular Christ, our mediator. Mary, for example, cannot touch the risen Savior until His mission is fully accomplished: "Jesus saith unto her, Touch me not; for I am not yet ascended to my Father: but go to my brethren, and say unto them, I ascend unto my Father, and your Father; and *to* my God, and your God" (John 20:17).

We are not to touch our holy Mediator nor do anything other than lovingly adore and seek to obey Him, following His every word and striving to put into practice everything that comes from His mouth. To go another way, to question this, to presumptuously seek to 'touch' God without going through the Mediator is tantamount to petulance and a shaking of one's fist at Him; for this we ought indeed to "perish" (Exod 19:21). To return in heart to Egypt and adopt worldly thoughts, words, tendencies, and fashions is abhorrent in God's eyes. While called to be separate, holy, rejoicing in a privileged sense of servanthood, if we would instead rather be our own 'gods' and effectively trample the Savior under foot then we are effectively putting "him to an open shame" (Heb 6:6), and deserve the LORD to "break forth upon" us (Exod 19:22).

Our God is no hard taskmaster like the masters of this cruel, slavish world system, typified by Egypt. He is a God of absolutes; fair and just, a holy, loving Father who wants the best for His children and who is training us in ways which will redound to our eternal good: "But that which beareth thorns and briers *is* rejected, and *is* nigh unto cursing; whose end *is* to be burned. But, beloved, we are persuaded better things of you, and things that accompany salvation, though we thus speak" (Heb 6:8–9). Woe betide any so-called pastor or minister of God who endeavors to drive a dispensational wedge between "the goodness and severity of God" (Rom 11:22).

# Exodus 19

## VERSES UPON WHICH TO MEDITATE

*(ideally in each chapter's context)*

### 1 Kings 4:34

And there came of all people to hear the wisdom of Solomon, from all kings of the earth, which had heard of his wisdom.

### John 20:17

Jesus saith unto her, Touch me not; for I am not yet ascended to my Father: but go to my brethren, and say unto them, I ascend unto my Father, and your Father; and *to* my God, and your God.

### Romans 10:6–7

But the righteousness which is of faith speaketh on this wise, Say not in thine heart, Who shall ascend into heaven? (that is, to bring Christ down *from above*:)

Or, Who shall descend into the deep? (that is, to bring up Christ again from the dead.)

### 1 Corinthians 3:23

And ye are Christ's; and Christ *is* God's.

### 1 Timothy 2:5

For *there is* one God, and one mediator between God and men, the man Christ Jesus;

### *Hebrews 6:6, 8–9*

If they shall fall away, to renew them again unto repentance; seeing they crucify to themselves the Son of God afresh, and put *him* to an open shame.

But that which beareth thorns and briers *is* rejected, and *is* nigh unto cursing; whose end *is* to be burned.

But, beloved, we are persuaded better things of you, and things that accompany salvation, though we thus speak.

### *10:31*

*It is* a fearful thing to fall into the hands of the living God.

## And Moses Went Up

The time had come for God to show
how far His people had to go,
as eagles' wings had borne them here,
so now to one He would appear.

A priestly kingdom they should be
a holy nation, shining, free,
to follow and adore His plan
to tell the word of God to man.

And so He came in thunder, fire
the people quaking with desire,
not one daring to approach
not one devoid of self-reproach.

Moses the mediator went
to spend his life and to be spent,
a chosen man called through God's fence
only in Christ his confidence.

# Exodus 20

SUCH A WELL-KNOWN PORTION of Scripture can best be understood if placed side by side our Lord's Sermon on the Mount, the ultimate fulfillment and practical explanation of what it means to live out the Law as a forgiven soul, in love with God and man. In this sense, it is not just a fear of thunder and lightning which so overwhelms the people but an overpowering sense of His holiness/human sinfulness. We might be reminded of Peter's confession to Jesus: "When Simon Peter saw *it*, he fell down at Jesus' knees, saying, Depart from me; for I am a sinful man, O Lord" (Luke 5:8). In this sense it is our inability to walk uprightly with God which turns us away from Him, our weakness and failings the things which render us desirous of dwelling at a more manageable distance. We know ourselves most truly when God reveals something of Himself to us; our sinfulness is then more fully exposed in its rank ugliness.

The moral law was not designed merely to frighten and scare, as Moses explains: "And Moses said unto the people, Fear not: for God is come to prove you, and that his fear may be before your faces, that ye sin not" (Exod 20:20). The Lord's will is for His image-bearers to live a holy and righteous life, in awe of His power, provision, and Fatherly involvement. Because of the intense incompatibility of a holy Creator with the fallen creature, our first instinct is to flee God's presence and become occupied with creaturely endeavor: "Then said they unto him, What shall we do, that we might work the works of God?" (John 6:28). These particular Israelites, we might remember, had for hundreds of years been surrounded by the amazing architecture and visions of worldly Egyptian minds, and so would naturally have wanted to respond to God by fashioning out their own similarly beautiful "gods of silver" and "gods of gold" (Exod 20:23). Religious man wants to have a hand in shaping his religion in "hewn stone" (20:25) and ornately created "steps" (v.26), the Vatican of our day being a prime example.

But God will not accept the handiwork of worldliness to bring about the advancement of His holy kingdom. Man must take a back seat, resisting the urge to add to or take away from God's glory: "This is the work of God, that ye believe on him whom he hath sent" (John 6:29). Our job is to receive, to bow down, to serve, to marvel, and to follow God's ways, not our own. To use a modern analogy, we are like an old, failing car which has been given a new, supersonic engine. Our job is not to meddle with such an unspeakable gift, but simply to trust that it will take us to places we never could have gone if we had used our own, faltering machinery.

Another remarkable thing to note is that such gracious provision for man's failure was made immediately *after* the legal proclamation of that which is owed to the Creator by the creature. The altar foreshadowing Christ's final and ultimate sacrifice of Himself came straight *after* the all-encompassing commandments of heart obedience to God's attributes and righteous expectations. Although the moral law was given so that we might "sin not" (Exod 20:20), God knew that we would sin and so provided a way for us to look upon His law as both a spur to holy obedience, and a high and holy thing that could only be approached through a Mediator. If the "altar of earth" represents the humanity of Jesus—His identification with our feeble flesh in every aspect bar sin, the "altar of stone" represents the Godhood of our Lord Jesus—His immovable, unalterable essence. Without the former we can have no hope of mercy, no substitute suitable to represent us and take our place; without the latter we can have no hope of justice, no assurance that those who repent will assuredly be saved, those who rebel divinely judged.

God is all things to us; He walked as one of us and yet dwells far, far above us, where "Eye hath not seen, nor ear heard, neither have entered into the heart of man, the things which God hath prepared for them that love him" (1 Cor 2:9). His proving of us is to train and wean us away from trust in this world and its kingdom of self, into humble dependence upon the 'strong meat' of His word: "But God hath revealed *them* unto us by his Spirit: for the Spirit searcheth all things, yea, the deep things of God" (1 Cor 2:10). It takes a lifetime to grow as a Christian, and yet in an instant all our learning and struggling will be resolved the very moment we leave this world and enter into our Father's glorious presence.

## VERSES UPON WHICH TO MEDITATE

*(ideally in each chapter's context)*

### Luke 5:8

When Simon Peter saw *it*, he fell down at Jesus' knees, saying, Depart from me; for I am a sinful man, O Lord.

### John 6:28-29

Then said they unto him, What shall we do, that we might work the works of God?

Jesus answered and said unto them, This is the work of God, that ye believe on him whom he hath sent.

### 1 Corinthians 2:9-10

But as it is written, Eye hath not seen, nor ear heard, neither have entered into the heart of man, the things which God hath prepared for them that love him.

But God hath revealed *them* unto us by his Spirit: for the Spirit searcheth all things, yea, the deep things of God.

## And the People Stood Afar Off

The Law was declared and mankind stood afar,
each soul could not keep it, each step could but mar,
the Law is a schoolteacher showing our sin
to drive men to hell or to Jesus made sin.

An altar of earth and an altar of stone
the blood of the Savior alone can atone,
an altar of stone and an altar of earth
Christ's body alone lived a life heaven worth.

No 'god' made of silver, no 'god' made of gold
can raise from the dead—only Christ can unfold,
no 'god' made of gold or of silver thus wrought
can bring to repentance those God hath not brought.

The Law is of God, it is holy and pure
our righteousness rubbish, our good deeds manure
one day we will dwell with Him, stripped of all fear
the Judge is the Savior—to Him we are dear.

# Exodus 21

TO OUR MODERN EARS much of this chapter seems distasteful. The Lord was dealing, after all, with a mass of people most of whom were not saved or called out in that spiritual sense. The more distilled version of this mixed multitude would not be seen until the inter-national church age of Jesus Christ, foreshadowed in so many places (Micah 4 being a prime example), to which the purer instructions of godly living were reserved as 'the good wine'—poured into that most blessed Sermon on the Mount. In this ancient time and place the Lord was preparing a cruder, less refined national instrument for His purposes. Thus we have such things as slavery, not of the inhumane transatlantic kind but rather bondservanthood or, as we might interpret it, bankruptcy leading a man to cast himself upon the mercy of a richer man for employment and protection.

There were also various rules about marriage, polygamy, criminal violence, and appropriate justice. This is a no holds barred, practical outworking of the second table of God's moral law delivered in the previous chapter, in particular commandment VI. At this time and in this place the practical outworking would take this form. However, throughout subsequent millenia and countries in which Christianity would take root such judicial legislations would cease to be, the ethnic theocracy of Israel now fulfilled and subsumed into the global *ekklesia* of Christ.

In terms of the post-exodus narrative of redemption, then, the believer is depicted as a bankrupt man, one who can say of Jesus Christ "I love my master", and "I will not go out free" (v.5). As with the apostle Paul's introductions to his God-breathed epistles so many centuries later, we see that a believer is a willing bondservant of Christ, one who sees the excellencies and supremacy of his heavenly Master and will seek not to serve another, not even *self*. It is interesting that it is not the lip or the tongue or indeed any other body part which needs be pierced, but "his ear" (v.6), for "faith *cometh* by hearing, and hearing by the word of God" (Rom 10:17). The prospect of being with Christ, to "serve him for ever" (Exod 21:6) delights the believer just as much as it appalls the atheist. Such is the nature of the two kingdoms—this world's and God's; members of this world's kingdom are deluded into thinking they serve no one or serve themselves, when in fact they are serving the devil, doing *his* will!

And there is also the contrast between the weak and uncaring polygamist ("If he take him another *wife*; her food, her raiment, and her duty of marriage, shall he not diminish" v. 10), and the faithful and loving God who has made provision for the "barren" gentile world (Isa 54:1) to be incorporated within His enlarged "tent" (v.2) of salvific blessing so as "not" to "be ashamed" (v.4), and to know her Maker as her "husband" (v.5). How much this has been the spirit of selfless missionaries and evangelists throughout the ages, and how contrary it has been to the narrow spirit of racial, colonial conquest characterizing man-made imperial might.

God is fair where fallen man is cruel and unkind. Even the punishment of unbelievers in hell is in proportion to their wickedness upon this earth: "many *stripes* . . . few *stripes*" (Luke 12:47–48). So it is in a foreshadowed form in this chapter, whereby the punishment must fit the crime: "life for life, eye for eye, tooth for tooth, hand for hand, foot for foot" (Exod 21:23–24). In our own day in the West there is no punishment for abortion, while in many places in the world extreme, cruel punishment for lack of adherence to the party line, be it religious or secular. Our God is a kind and fair God, one who would go on to impute Christ's perfect, blameless, undefiled, holy life, to *our* sin-filled, corrupt, self-seeking rebel's life, the Sinless taking the punishment of the sinful upon Himself.

While the world is intent on not punishing real wickedness and overpunishing perceived wickedness, the divine balance is found in Christ alone. We ought to meditate more upon the fact that He died for us not while we were repenting or striving to be forgiven, but "while we were yet sinners" (Rom 5:8). While we were unjustly punishing HIS non-existent wickedness, deriding HIM in His hour of agony, God the Son was asking God the Father to "forgive them, for they know not what they do" (Luke 23:34), them being the human race including us. Praised be His name.

## VERSES UPON WHICH TO MEDITATE

*(ideally in each chapter's context)*

### Isaiah 54:1-2, 4-5

Sing, O barren, thou *that* didst not bear; break forth into singing, and cry aloud, thou *that* didst not travail with child: for more *are* the children of the desolate than the children of the married wife, saith the LORD.

Enlarge the place of thy tent, and let them stretch forth the curtains of thine habitations: spare not, lengthen thy cords, and strengthen thy stakes;

Fear not; for thou shalt not be ashamed: neither be thou confounded; for thou shalt not be put to shame: for thou shalt forget the shame of thy youth, and shalt not remember the reproach of thy widowhood any more.

For thy Maker *is* thine husband; the LORD of hosts *is* his name; and thy Redeemer the Holy One of Israel; The God of the whole earth shall he be called.

### Luke 12:47-48

And that servant, which knew his lord's will, and prepared not *himself*, neither did according to his will, shall be beaten with many *stripes*.

But he that knew not, and did commit things worthy of stripes, shall be beaten with few *stripes*. For unto whomsoever much is given, of him shall be much required: and to whom men have committed much, of him they will ask the more.

### 23:34

Then said Jesus, Father, forgive them; for they know not what they do. And they parted his raiment, and cast lots.

## Romans 5:8

But God commendeth his love toward us, in that, while we were yet sinners, Christ died for us.

### 10:17

So then faith *cometh* by hearing, and hearing by the word of God.

## And He Shall Serve Him for Ever

That world a world of hatred, lust
polygamy and slavery,
one nation would the Lord entrust
with laws to teach, altars to free.

Israel a theocratic state
a mass, a mixèd multitude,
all nations hate all nations—hate!
so God addressed this attitude.

God called them to be kind with kind
to love the servant, love the wife,
for cruelty is not of God's mind
though Satan hates each human life.

This prototype of Christian church
drawn out from Egypt's darkest veins,
deaf ones God's word would fain besmirch
while loved ones' ears did take great pains.

# Exodus 22

How different the Lord's instructions with regard to His VIIIth commandment from our contemporary world which goes to ungodly extremes. In certain countries of our day the severing of limbs is the punishment for stealing, whilst in modern Britain there is now all but no punishment for theft under a certain amount of money! With God every detail matters and the punishment will fit the crime. To steal and be caught generally led to a restitution of double: "he shall restore double" (Exod 22:4), but the chapter reaches a climax with the concept of stealing from God ("Thou shalt not delay *to offer* the first of thy ripe fruits" v. 29).

Thus the New Testament Christian is to learn not only to do no wrong, but also positively to do right. Our calling is to be, in Christ, sin-free and active workers of righteousness, "For we are his workmanship, created in Christ Jesus unto good works, which God hath before ordained that we should walk in them" (Eph 2:10). This is not an added burden put upon us but rather the privilege of being a citizen of heaven, our "reasonable service" (Rom 12:1).

There is, under this umbrella VIIIth commandment, the outworking of all kinds of theft and various kinds of thieves. There is the obvious stealer or withholder of property in verses 1–15. Then there are the less obvious examples of the fornicator (Exod 22:16), the communer with demonic forces (v.18), the committer of bestiality (v.19), the idolater (v. 20), and the oppressor of various kinds or types of believer (v. 21–28); these types of believer in verses 21–28 being of much interest in that they explore different facets of the Christian from various angles, like the rotation of a precious gem.

There is the "stranger" (v. 21) which reflects both Israel's own formation and preservation in the oppressive, aesthetically emphatic land of Egypt, and yet which also foreshadows Christian believers who were once worldlings, "without Christ, being aliens from the commonwealth of Israel, and strangers from the covenants of promise" (Eph 2:12). There is the "widow" (Exod 22:22) who typifies the gentile world spoken of in Isaiah 54 ("Sing! O barren . . . and shalt not remember the reproach of thy widowhood any more"). Then there is the "fatherless child" (Exod 22:22) which represents the spiritually bereft sinner who may now call upon God his/her father: "At that day ye shall know that I *am* in my Father, and ye in me, and I in you" (John 14:20).

There is the "poor" (Exod 22:25), which points ultimately to the Lord Jesus—"for your sakes he became poor, that ye through his poverty might be rich" (2 Cor 8:9). There is the homeless (Exod 22:26–27) whose home is now "with all spiritual blessings in heavenly *places* in Christ" (Eph 1:3). And, rather than confusion or communism there is God-appointed leadership ordained for our good, prefigured in the "gods" or rather "judges" of v. 28; we are to give thanks and pray for "kings, and *for* all that are in authority" (1 Tim 2:2), and honor the "bishop" or overseer ("If a man desire the office of a bishop, he desireth a good work" 1 Tim 3:1), and the deacons (v. 8), and "the elders that rule well" (1 Tim 5:17), and "the aged women" (Titus 2:3).

All of these things belong somewhere under the VIIIth commandment and are to lead us to "be holy men" (Exod 22:31) and women, rejoicing in Christ through whom our shameful thefts and departures from God's perfect ways have been atoned, our paths of sanctification paved with His everlasting love.

# Exodus 22

## VERSES UPON WHICH TO MEDITATE

*(ideally in each chapter's context)*

### *Isaiah 54:1, 4*

Sing, O barren, thou *that* didst not bear; break forth into singing, and cry aloud, thou *that* didst not travail with child: for more *are* the children of the desolate than the children of the married wife, saith the LORD.

Fear not; for thou shalt not be ashamed: neither be thou confounded; for thou shalt not be put to shame: for thou shalt forget the shame of thy youth, and shalt not remember the reproach of thy widowhood any more.

### *John 14:20*

At that day ye shall know that I *am* in my Father, and ye in me, and I in you.

### *Romans 12:1*

I beseech you therefore, brethren, by the mercies of God, that ye present your bodies a living sacrifice, holy, acceptable unto God, *which is* your reasonable service.

### *2 Corinthians 8:9*

For ye know the grace of our Lord Jesus Christ, that, though he was rich, yet for your sakes he became poor, that ye through his poverty might be rich.

### *Ephesians 1:3*

Blessed *be* the God and Father of our Lord Jesus Christ, who hath blessed us with all spiritual blessings in heavenly *places* in Christ:

### 2:10, 12

For we are his workmanship, created in Christ Jesus unto good works, which God hath before ordained that we should walk in them.

That at that time ye were without Christ, being aliens from the commonwealth of Israel, and strangers from the covenants of promise, having no hope, and without God in the world:

### 1 Timothy 2:2

For kings, and *for* all that are in authority; that we may lead a quiet and peaceable life in all godliness and honesty.

### 3:1, 8

This *is* a true saying, If a man desire the office of a bishop, he desireth a good work.

Likewise *must* the deacons be grave, not doubletongued, not given to much wine, not greedy of filthy lucre;

### 5:17

Let the elders that rule well be counted worthy of double honour, especially they who labour in the word and doctrine.

### Titus 2:3

The aged women likewise, that *they be* in behaviour as becometh holiness, not false accusers, not given to much wine, teachers of good things;

## And Ye Shall Be Holy Men before Me

I owe my God my body, soul
sins done, righteousnesses undone,
I owe God all, not part, my whole
for not one thing is mine, not one.

For Jesus paid me more than double
paid my debt, rendered me righteous,
yet I daily bring Him trouble
still in Him dwell as Him righteous!

God's virgins, vagrants, each, all
have life beyond this mortal realm,
as orphans, widows, were we all
until God-man stood at the helm.

Will we therefore for profit live
holding back offerings, hoarding stuff?
trying to steal what He does give,
is Christ our treasure not enough?

# Exodus 23

THIS CHAPTER DIVIDES INTO two halves; the first concerning the practical outworking of commandments IX and IV, respectively, then the way in which God's people are to approach Him; through repentance from the leaven of sin ("leavened bread" Exod 23:18), and faith in the promised, crucified Seed of the woman ("the blood of my sacrifice" v.18). Only then can our fruit be deemed acceptable, worthy of being an offering ("The first of the firstfruits" v.19) to the Almighty. In other words, all attempts to deviate from or dilute the plain Gospel are doomed to become "a snare unto thee" (v.33).

The second half of this chapter maps out the life of sanctification in which we are not expected to go our own way but are jealously provided for and protected by "an Angel" (v.20), none other than a theophany of the Lord Jesus, "for my name is in him" (v.21). They were and we are to love and to cherish Him because He loved and would die for them and us in the fullness of time. We do not merely know Him as a theory but "know his voice" (John 10:4), it being their chief desire to "obey his voice" (Exod 23:22), our heavenly Father declaring that "This is my beloved Son: hear him" (Luke 9:35), the Holy Spirit lovingly warning us to "refuse not him that speaketh" (Heb 12:25).

We have a holy war to wage and the forces of hell, flesh, and world to overcome. In our selves "we are accounted as sheep for the slaughter" (Rom 8:36) but strangely, gloriously "are more than conquerors through him that loved us" (v.37). In the context of Exodus 23 the enemies were "the Amorites, and the Hittites, and the Perizzites, and the Canaanites, the Hivites, and the Jebusites" (v.23). In the context of our times it is the powerfully seductive ideas of militant atheism, nominal Christianity, misandrous feminism, Islamic Jihad, bigoted Hindu nationalism, dehumanizing communism, bullying Buddhism, and the list goes on. We are not to fear what man can do for man cannot touch the soul.

Curiously, the Lord reveals how "By little and little I will drive them out from before thee" (v.30), for the life of justification happens quickly but the life of sanctification slowly unfolds. The Lord Jesus explains that "I have yet many things to say unto you, but ye cannot bear them now" (John 16:12). To have to endure the trials and carry the weight of expectations that a seasoned believer has been prepared for might well crush an unseasoned "novice" (1 Tim 3:6) and make "shipwreck" (1 Tim 1:19) of the faith of a 'new born'. The people of God in Exodus would not be ready to undertake all the challenges of holy warfare until the book of Joshua. Likewise, Christian believers are challenged to "walk in the Spirit" in order that they "live in the Spirit" (Gal 5:25). Just as they spent in some cases a lifetime learning to mimic the devil, they need another lifetime to appreciate and work out what they now are in Christ.

In the chapters ahead we know so well the trials, disappointments, and successes of the people of God in this era. We too are being tested, disciplined, and sometimes "chastened", not because God is against us but because He is our loving heavenly Father. He knows exactly what we need and when we need it, so that the "peaceable fruit of righteousness" (Heb 12:11) might be ours. We may with much profit meditate upon the struggles of the Christian life shown in Romans 7, but it is our destiny to dwell increasingly upon the victories of the Christian life shown in Romans 8. Equally, Exodus 23 is preparing us for the transcendent, unspeakable glory that awaits us in Exodus 24.

## VERSES UPON WHICH TO MEDITATE

*(ideally in each chapter's context)*

### *Luke 9:35*

And there came a voice out of the cloud, saying, This is my beloved Son: hear him.

### *John 10:4*

And when he putteth forth his own sheep, he goeth before them, and the sheep follow him: for they know his voice.

### *16:12*

I have yet many things to say unto you, but ye cannot bear them now.

### *Romans 8:36-37*

As it is written, For thy sake we are killed all the day long; we are accounted as sheep for the slaughter.

Nay, in all these things we are more than conquerors through him that loved us.

### *Galatians 5:25*

If we live in the Spirit, let us also walk in the Spirit.

### *1 Timothy 1:19*

Holding faith, and a good conscience; which some having put away concerning faith have made shipwreck:

### 3:6

Not a novice, lest being lifted up with pride he fall into the condemnation of the devil.

### Hebrews 12:11, 25

Now no chastening for the present seemeth to be joyous, but grievous: nevertheless afterward it yieldeth the peaceable fruit of righteousness unto them which are exercised thereby.

See that ye refuse not him that speaketh. For if they escaped not who refused him that spake on earth, much more *shall not we escape*, if we turn away from him that *speaketh* from heaven:

## By Little and Little

What soul can keep its witness true
be in the world but of the Lord,
what Christian loves the stranger too
as much as those of family chord.

What soul fulfils the Sabbath day
thinking not of work, pleasure, self,
what Christian leaves all else to pray
cares, riches, lusts left on the shelf.

What soul dare come into God's rest
with even one sin kept intact,
what Christian won't give God the best
worshipping lukewarm, cold, in fact.

The Angel of the Lord must keep
His chosen people on the path,
our Chief Commander rouse from sleep
us waning watchmen, saved from wrath.

# Exodus 24

WE ARE REMINDED HERE of just how personal and intimate God's dealings with us are. Just as there is a public display of God to the assembled church, there is also the intensely private and individual communion of the believer with his/her heavenly Father. As a type of Christ one is reminded here of Christ's farewell discourse of John 14–17 in which He speaks of things too great for us to fully fathom this side of eternity. However, as a type of believer Moses represents the *closet* meditations of a soul which retreats from the world into the word of God and prayer. We cannot fully attain unto these things whilst we are in company, even good Christian company; it is the solitary and holy communion with God which is here typified.

God is in 'union' with souls in a gathered church of believers at any given moment of time, as they fellowship with one another and "eat and drink" (Exod 24:11) in His presence, giving thanks for all things in His name. However, God is more perfectly realized, more deeply in communion with the soul which seeks to dwell in His presence in a more intense, meditative way: "And the LORD said unto Moses, Come up to me into the mount, and be there" (v.12). It is not only the seeking of God which bears fruit within the believer's life so much as the desire to *be there*—with God; abiding in Him and not having anything higher on the agenda than Him.

There should be a time in a believer's life which marks the graduation from infancy "milk" to more robust "meat" (1 Cor 3:2). The believer's life is not static, and through Christ we are granted a growing appetite and capacity for the deeper dimensions of His perfect moral law: "tables of stone, and a law, and commandments which I have written", with a view to us being of use to others: "that thou mayest teach them" (Exod 24:12). Each believer is thus navigating the narrow way; to the novice or immature those more seasoned giants of the faith may seem to be living at a distance, further on, which may seem like "devouring fire on the top of the mount" (v.17).

Like the disciples of Jesus some millennium and a half later, there was fear among them ("they fell on their face" Matt 17:6) as they started to appreciate the magnitude of the transfiguration and what it might mean for their lives. And yet the key for all Christians, whether starting out or advanced in the faith, is to keep one's eyes upon that which is precious, essential, and truly good: "And when they had lifted up their eyes, they saw no man, save Jesus only" (Matt 17:8). He may have saved us, yes, but He will also *keep* us along life's way, praised be His name.

Let us each take note of the glorious heights to which Moses was called, and see that for us it means to "enter into thy closet" (Matt 6:6) and be prayerfully welling up with the love of God in our hearts, which should be animating and motivating our every daily intention and domestic interaction: "and then shall he have rejoicing in himself alone, and not in another" (Gal 6:4). We may never truly know each other as we know ourselves, "for the heart knoweth his own bitterness; and a stranger doth not intermeddle with his joy" (Prov 14:10), but our Father in heaven knows us, each and every one, while He actively and passively answers our prayers for His glory, according to His will. May we be more willing to be a little bit more devotionally inward, so "thy Father which seeth in secret shall reward thee openly" (Matt 6:6).

# EXODUS 24

## VERSES UPON WHICH TO MEDITATE

*(ideally in each chapter's context)*

### Proverbs 14:10

The heart knoweth his own bitterness; and a stranger doth not intermeddle with his joy.

### Matthew 6:6

But thou, when thou prayest, enter into thy closet, and when thou hast shut thy door, pray to thy Father which is in secret; and thy Father which seeth in secret shall reward thee openly.

### 17:6, 8

And when the disciples heard it, they fell on their face, and were sore afraid.

And when they had lifted up their eyes, they saw no man, save Jesus only.

### 1 Corinthians 3:2

I have fed you with milk, and not with meat: for hitherto ye were not able *to bear it*, neither yet now are ye able.

### Galatians 6:4

But let every man prove his own work, and then shall he have rejoicing in himself alone, and not in another.

## And a Cloud Covered the Mount

A type of Christ was Moses, drawn
to go on up to God alone,
for for God's glory was he born
though Jesus would for him atone.

The words he wrote were God's not his
the blood bespeaking Calvary,
the sinner must confront God's justice
flee to Christ, for God can't vary.

Then the vision pre-incarnate
heaven poured into their eyes,
their souls and bodies satiate
were made to worship, realize.

And Moses, Christ in type, was bid
to rise up into sacred cloud
for we are dead, in Christ are hid
He deals with souls away from crowd.

# Exodus 25

WHEREVER THERE IS GOD'S holy and specific blueprint for humanity, there is a grotesque and worldly counterfeit lurking in the rebel's heart. Where our first parents were presented with a paradise, Lucifer fueled their desire for another (false) one. Where Noah was divinely commissioned to spend the best part of a century methodically building an ark and preaching God's word, his descendants presumptuously erected a tower of Babel in order to promote their own glory. And where Moses is commanded to build a tabernacle "according to all that I show thee" (Exod 25:9) with vessels made "after their pattern which was shown thee in the mount" (v.40), in a short space of time Aaron would be peer pressured into making an abominable molten calf!

In the structurally symbolic details of Scripture, Christ the Lord is foreshadowed and glorified: "But he spake of the temple of his body" (John 2:21). We ignore such things at our peril, to the detriment of ongoing sanctification. We dare not give God's glory to a person, to a denomination, or to a building; it belongs to Him and every jot and tittle of Scripture attests to it, it being "the glory of God to conceal a thing: but the honour of kings . . . to search out a matter" (Prov 25:2). Thus, the exacting details of Scripture are as worthy of investigation as its overall themes and promises.

The colors of verses 3–7 have been well discussed by the likes of M.R Dehaan, A.W. Pink, and others; one other thing to note being the voluntary principle whereby God is most honored and glorified when believers joyfully center their lives upon Him, bringing their worship and offering "willingly", from the "heart" (Exod 25:2). We too should be bringing our worship with us into church on a Sunday, rather than distractedly and dutifully being there in body, not in spirit. It is profitable also to align Christ as "the way, the truth, and the life" in John 14:6 with Hebrews 9:2–4, in which we see the divinely inspired order of "the candlestick . . . the table . . . the ark . . ."

## Departures

Christ is our *way* for without Him we walk in darkness, yet in His "light shall we see light" (Ps 36:9). His *way* is infinitely superior to our way, His word a source of never-ending wonder, utterly unlike the works of a Shakespeare or an Aristotle. In fact, *a* way of beauty, splendor, and worldly excitement would soon come to rival God's quiet, hallowed way, in the form of an obnoxiously crass golden calf; yet what emptiness and vanity it would reveal, opposed as it was to the inward tranquility and meditative power of the "candlestick *of* pure gold" (Exod 25:31).

He is also the *truth* of our existence, for we cannot consistently dwell upon the mountain-top in our daily pilgrimage but must needs have our horizontal, man-ward relationships, our eating, our drinking, our "dishes", our "spoons", our "bowls", and our "showbread" (v.29–30). Whatever we do we want to do for God's glory, and so He makes His *truth* practicable and dwells in the midst of us, enclosing us with "a golden crown to the border thereof round about" (v.25). Whether Christian is with Christian, or alone, or with colleagues in secular employment, the Lord is with His people "in spirit and in truth" (John 4:24), ever ready to "sup with him, and he with me" (Rev 3:20) because He is the *truth*, and without Him we fall into error.

The ark is a fuller type of Christ Jesus our Lord and Savior, for in this "Holiest of all" places (Heb 9:3) none other than He is the meeting-place in which "I will meet with thee, and I will commune with thee from above the mercy seat" (Exod 25:22). He is both God ("pure gold" v.11) and man ("shittim wood" v.10), sitting upon the throne amid the ministering angels ("from between the two cherubim" v. 22); without His atoning work at Calvary whereby He crushed the devil, we would all be judged by His Law. Only in Christ can there be peace between wretched rebels and a perfect, holy God. He is the *life*, and when the *way* and the *truth* have served their pilgrims' progress He will remain our *life* for all eternity, "For Christ is not entered into the holy places made with hands, *which* are the figures of the true; but into heaven itself, now to appear in the presence of God for us" (Heb 9:24), He being "the resurrection, and the life" (John 11:25).

Others have deeply pondered on such wondrous things, and have seen much richness and many facets of the person and work of our great High Priest. May we similarly seek to apply ourselves assiduously to the details of the word of God, in order that we may set our "affection" increasingly upon "things above, not on things on the earth" (Col 3:2). The details of the Tabernacle were first revealed to Moses by God *before* He then commanded him to inscripturate them for His glory and our good. May we not fall into *a* way, *a* truth, or *a* life which is counterfeit and of the devil, for he is not to be underestimated and has thousands of years' experience tempting, luring and bedazzling religious folk with "signs and lying wonders" (2 Thess 2:9).

DEPARTURES

# VERSES UPON WHICH TO MEDITATE

*(ideally in each chapter's context)*

### *Psalm 36:9*

For with thee *is* the fountain of life: in thy light shall we see light.

### *Proverbs 25:2*

*It is* the glory of God to conceal a thing: but the honour of kings *is* to search out a matter.

### *John 2:21*

But he spake of the temple of his body.

### *4:24*

God *is* a Spirit: and they that worship him must worship *him* in spirit and in truth.

### *11:25*

Jesus said unto her, I am the resurrection, and the life: he that believeth in me, though he were dead, yet shall he live:

### *14:6, 24*

Jesus saith unto him, I am the way, the truth, and the life: no man cometh unto the Father, but by me.

He that loveth me not keepeth not my sayings: and the word which ye hear is not mine, but the Father's which sent me.

# Exodus 25

### Colossians 3:2

Set your affection on things above, not on things on the earth.

### 2 Thessalonians 2:9

*Even him*, whose coming is after the working of Satan with all power and signs and lying wonders,

### Hebrews 9:2-4, 24

For there was a tabernacle made; the first, wherein was the candlestick, and the table, and the shewbread; which is called the sanctuary.

And after the second veil, the tabernacle which is called the Holiest of all;

Which had the golden censer, and the ark of the covenant overlaid round about with gold, wherein was the golden pot that had manna, and Aaron's rod that budded, and the tables of the covenant;

For Christ is not entered into the holy places made with hands, *which are* the figures of the true; but into heaven itself, now to appear in the presence of God for us:

### Revelation 3:20

Behold, I stand at the door, and knock: if any man hear my voice, and open the door, I will come in to him, and will sup with him, and he with me.

## According to All That I Show Thee

From earth to heaven we can't go
so God brings earth heaven to show
inside His tabernacle dwell
all souls believing, saved from hell.

The ark of gold bespeaketh Jesus
God-man dwells with, ever sees us,
reigning from His mercy seat
the law fulfilled, beneath His feet.

A table He prepares for all
who're resurrected from the Fall,
who feed on Him and never frown
while shunning crowns, all for His crown.

He gives us light as He is light
the source of every pure delight,
without Him souls may clamber in
yet still benighted, be in sin.

# Exodus 26

AT REGULAR INTERVALS GOD through Moses reminds us that His particular and internally magnificent details were *revealed* to Moses, not originated by him: "And thou shalt rear up the tabernacle according to the fashion thereof which was shewed thee in the mount" (Exod 26:30). Similarly, our precious Bibles are not the relics of human speculation, for "holy men of God spake as they were moved by the Holy Ghost" (2 Pet 1:21), and hell awaits any who would presumptuously seek to "add unto" or "take from" (Rev 22:18–19) it. Speaking reverently, Moses would have been removed if, as God's chosen servant, he had willfully sought to corrupt or alter one jot or tittle of God's holy plan for His tabernacle.

Moses could not glory in self, for everything he conveyed to the architects, smiths, and master craftsmen of Israel had the ring of divine truth and was revealed rather than personally decided on. So too is our conversion "not of works, lest any man should boast" (Eph 2:9); rather, "we are his workmanship" (v.10), not in any way skilled, original practitioners of extraordinary genius. The world has its Nobel Prize winners, Olympic gold medalists, and Oscar nominees, but the Bible its humbled, submitting servants of God; chosen messengers of a higher order in which man can take not one iota of credit. No wonder the world seeks to minimize and bypass it, for therein dwells nothing praiseworthy to the flesh.

Interestingly, God again uses the rule of three in order to furnish and decorate His holy structure; the "goats' hair" (Exod 26:7)—"rams' skins"—"badgers' skins" (v.14) reflecting various facets of Christ. God's justice was to be satisfied through the scape-*goat* of a perfect substitute, God's strength (the ram) was perfected in weakness, for how else could He have dwelt as a man without being instantaneously destroyed by His overpowering glory. God's humility put man's humility to shame, for what man among us would die for his friends let alone his enemies, the badger such a lowly and servile creature by comparison with even the goat or the ram.

Gold, silver, and brass reflect the Divinity, the blood, and the suffering of Jesus on our behalf. Where the Olympic or Oscar gold symbolizes what man tends to think of himself, the God-man would allow Himself to be put through the furnace of affliction in order that the dross of human sin might be dealt with, once and for all. Blue, purple, and scarlet represent Christ as Prophet, King, and Priest, who sacrificed Himself in order to deal with sin's awful consequence. And the curtains, the furniture, the veils, and all manner of other details such as the numerology, all reflect something of our blessed Savior. Our God is a specific God, a Holy One who instructed Noah to perfection so that the ark could withstand a world of aquatic pressure. The Tabernacle was a mystery to the outside world—all the glory lay within.

To believers the three-fold structure of the Tabernacle represents levels of blessedness towards which to strive. Not only was the Tabernacle itself a mysterious and secretive entity, just as true Christianity is to the novice, but after taking an interest in it as a whole there was the "hanging for the door" (v.36) of justification, just as souls are beckoned to the "the door" of Jesus Christ (John 10:9), and must seek no other door of worldly construction. Further, we are reminded by the ensuing "vail . . . of cunning work: with cherubims" (Exod 26:31) that in the Christian's walk there is a division between "the holy *place* and the most holy" (v.33). Only in private devotions and quiet meditations do we have access to that deeper, more intimate communion with God, for it is the will of God for believers to grow in grace in order to "be with me where I am; that they may behold my glory, which thou hast given me" (John 17:24).

The three-fold elements of the Tabernacle thus remind us how impossible such meditation and prayer is whilst we dwell in the hurly-burly of daily necessities and fleshly responsibilities. It is a reminder for us to slow down, take time out, and treat our quiet times seriously and reverentially, remembering the holiness of the One with whom we have to do.

# Exodus 26

## VERSES UPON WHICH TO MEDITATE

*(ideally in each chapter's context)*

### John 10:9

I am the door: by me if any man enter in, he shall be saved, and shall go in and out, and find pasture.

### 17:24

Father, I will that they also, whom thou hast given me, be with me where I am; that they may behold my glory, which thou hast given me: for thou lovedst me before the foundation of the world.

### Ephesians 2:9-10

Not of works, lest any man should boast.

For we are his workmanship, created in Christ Jesus unto good works, which God hath before ordained that we should walk in them.

### 2 Peter 1:21

For the prophecy came not in old time by the will of man: but holy men of God spake *as they were* moved by the Holy Ghost.

### Revelation 22:18-19

For I testify unto every man that heareth the words of the prophecy of this book, If any man shall add unto these things, God shall add unto him the plagues that are written in this book:

And if any man shall take away from the words of the book of this prophecy, God shall take away his part out of the book of life, and out of the holy city, and *from* the things which are written in this book.

## According to the Fashion Thereof

Material and spiritual
the Lord is Lord of all,
the goats' hair, rams' and badgers' skin
portraying parts of sin.

The precious substances of man
but symbols of a higher plan,
gold speaks of God, blood silver shows
brass beaten, Calvary's furnace glows.

The veil entwined with cherubim
shows Eden's realm, now oh so dim,
the door's hanging of linen twined
prefiguring Jesus, human, kind.

Lord Christ—of blue and purple, scarlet
Prophet, King and Priest, our target,
worldly roads return to Rome
Lord Jesus, take us, Thou art Home.

# Exodus 27

THIS DIVINELY INSPIRED, HOLY structure has been revealed to us throughout the previous two chapters, from within to without. It is a picture of Christ, not a form of works salvation for the Bible knows of no such thing; from the clothing of Adam and Eve onwards salvation has been by grace. Those who believingly enter into Christ are saved, drawn as they are through the blue, purple, and scarlet of their Prophet, King, and Priest. To project forward, the Tabernacle as *type* is realized in the "by me if any man enter in, he shall be saved" (John 10:9). Sanctification, in terms of the finer details of the ministrations of the altar and the exact measurements and substances of true religion, has *already* been revealed, just as they were already revealed to Moses prior to their inscripturation for the benefit of millions throughout time. In this sense it is the daily entering in which is key, the details of which are worked out in prayer, according to God's omniscient plan.

And what has man done with such blessedly precise, Christ exalting details? Has he endeavored by faith to "enter into my rest" (Heb 4:5), rejoicing in the finished work of the Savior-King? Has he come to realize that he now has access to "the throne of grace" (v.16)? Has he striven to be among the "teachers" (Heb 5:12) of this fallen world, grasping the "strong meat" (v.14) of the Scriptures to the glory of God and benefit of man? Has he striven not to be "slothful" especially in the spiritual domain, so that he may become "followers of them who through faith and patience inherit the promises" (6:12)? Has he anchored himself in the One who has entered into the Holy of holies, "within the veil" (Heb 6:19)? Has he abandoned man-made works religion so as to submit to "an unchangeable priesthood" (7:24) with access to "a better covenant, which was established upon better promises" (8:6) in which Christ has finally "put away sin by the sacrifice of himself" (9:26)?

No . . . nowhere more clearly 'no' than in the so-called Holy Roman Catholic church, which has so cruelly and deceptively inverted the order of salvation so that this spiritual Tabernacle becomes a place of meritorious works, the priesthood of religious man remains intact, the individual soul is robbed of assurance of salvation with no direct access to the Savior-King, no hope of full and final forgiveness, no prospect of justification by faith alone, no entering into communion with Jesus, but a slow and painful false promise of works which may or may not lead to heaven. The same is seen with Islam's capricious and impersonal deity, Hinduism with its thousands of curiously distorted animal gods, Buddhism with its absence of anything tangible, and atheism with its fist-shaking defiance of God.

Moses was used instrumentally to erect a religious establishment "as it was shewed" him "in the mount" (Exod 27:8). Thousands of years later we are here, worshipping God "by a new and living way" (Heb 10:20), awaiting "the tabernacle of God" to descend, in which "he will dwell" (Rev 21:3) with us forever in a way that cannot destroyed by any marauding invaders fueled by devilish intent, or the indwelling sin that seeks to grow like weeds within.

In the meantime there is much to be done in terms of the details, as we who are saved by grace seek to work out our "own salvation with fear and trembling" (Phil 2:12). We utterly abhor any element of creature merit or personal goodness, but rather seek to be conduits through which the Lord will enact His sovereign plan for this fallen, sin-sick world: "For it is God which worketh in you both to will and to do of *his* good pleasure" (v.13).

# Exodus 27

## VERSES UPON WHICH TO MEDITATE

*(ideally in each chapter's context)*

### *John 10:9*

I am the door: by me if any man enter in, he shall be saved, and shall go in and out, and find pasture.

### *Philippians 2:12-13*

Wherefore, my beloved, as ye have always obeyed, not as in my presence only, but now much more in my absence, work out your own salvation with fear and trembling.

For it is God which worketh in you both to will and to do of *his* good pleasure.

### *Hebrews 4:5, 16*

And in this *place* again, If they shall enter into my rest.

Let us therefore come boldly unto the throne of grace, that we may obtain mercy, and find grace to help in time of need.

### *5:12, 14*

For when for the time ye ought to be teachers, ye have need that one teach you again which *be* the first principles of the oracles of God; and are become such as have need of milk, and not of strong meat.

But strong meat belongeth to them that are of full age, *even* those who by reason of use have their senses exercised to discern both good and evil.

### *6:12, 19*

That ye be not slothful, but followers of them who through faith and patience inherit the promises.

Which *hope* we have as an anchor of the soul, both sure and stedfast, and which entereth into that within the veil;

## *7:24*

But this *man*, because he continueth ever, hath an unchangeable priesthood.

## *8:6*

But now hath he obtained a more excellent ministry, by how much also he is the mediator of a better covenant, which was established upon better promises.

## *9:26*

For then must he often have suffered since the foundation of the world: but now once in the end of the world hath he appeared to put away sin by the sacrifice of himself.

## *10:20*

By a new and living way, which he hath consecrated for us, through the veil, that is to say, his flesh;

## *Revelation 21:3*

And I heard a great voice out of heaven saying, Behold, the tabernacle of God *is* with men, and he will dwell with them, and they shall be his people, and God himself shall be with them, *and be* their God.

## As It Was Shewed Thee in the Mount

The soul must enter through the gate
by faith forsaking all self rule,
leaving behind all worldly hate
all works religion, human, cruel.

Four corners had the altar horned
God's true religion, meant for all,
but Seed of woman would be scorned,
Christ shunning bitterness and gall.

The whole of Jesus, slain for us
One sacrifice, entire, complete,
no more rehearsals, vessels, fuss
the final Adam would defeat.

We have a holy tabernacle
God the Son Himself is it,
all Scripture's there for us to tackle,
Christ concealed, revealed through it.

# Exodus 28

JUST AS THE POST-FLOOD rainbow signifying God's covenant with mankind was a divinely bestowed marvel, so too the form of religion which is true and pleasing unto the Lord is beautiful, not in any way ugly. Upon the "breastplate of judgement" (Exod 28:15) the twelve precious stones were each most probably of particular symbolic importance, something about which C.W. Slemming has written with much insight in his book *These Are The Garments*. The anti-typical truth, moreover, is that our High Priest, the Lord Jesus Christ, has our names "upon his heart before the LORD continually" (v.30), even as we go about our daily business and weekly affairs with too often scarcely a thought for Him.

Lest we begin to accrue credit to the arm of flesh, the Lord reminds us that even the very best of man's religious observances; prayers, preaching, evangelism, care for the elderly and infirm "bear . . . iniquity" (v.38), and in and of themselves are impure without Christ's intercessory operation. Only through Him may we "be accepted before the LORD" (v.38) because we are "accepted in the beloved" (Eph 1:6) and *only* "in the beloved", not through any other avenue pre or post conversion.

It is of great interest that the "plate of pure gold" bearing the words "HOLINESS TO THE LORD" (Exod 28:36) was to be "upon Aaron's forehead" (v.38) because even this signifies Christ, "the head of the body, the church" (Col 1:18). Indeed, it is through our heads which we must trust, not through our hearts which are "deceitful above all *things*" (Jer 17:9). In the time of our conversion "the eyes of" our "understanding" were "enlightened" (Eph 1:18), and since that time it is "with the mind" that we "serve the law of God" (Rom 7:25), the heart being associated more with our passionate "members" which are so often "warring against the law of" one's enlightened "mind" (v.23).

Furthermore, the whole body of a believer is ruled by the head, and then in turn sanctified in every part; the "coats", the "girdles", the "bonnets" (Exod 28:40), and "linen breeches" (v. 42) reminding us that in Christ we are "clean through the word which" He has "spoken unto" us (John 15:3). Our feet, however, plod along the shifting, unclean sands of this world, and so while being regarded as clean in toto we still need daily repentance and cleansing from above, for "He that is washed needeth not save to wash his feet" (John 13:10).

Let us go about our lives regularly entering into the tabernacle of Jesus Christ—the heavenly realization of this earthly visual aid. May our prayers and thoughts be lively as "a golden bell and a pomegranate" (Exod 28:34) of repentance and rejoicing, that our "sound shall be heard" (v.35) by our Father in heaven, that we "bear not iniquity, and die" (v.43) for our thoughtless, ugly, dead orthodoxy. May we wonder and rejoice that Christ alone is described as having "a golden girdle" (Rev 1:13) not threaded or twined with other materials, for He alone is our true High Priest in glory.

## VERSES UPON WHICH TO MEDITATE

*(ideally in each chapter's context)*

### *Jeremiah 17:9*

The heart is deceitful above all *things*, and desperately wicked: who can know it?

### *John 13:10*

Jesus saith to him, He that is washed needeth not save to wash *his* feet, but is clean every whit: and ye are clean, but not all.

### *15:3*

Now ye are clean through the word which I have spoken unto you.

### *Romans 7:23, 25*

But I see another law in my members, warring against the law of my mind, and bringing me into captivity to the law of sin which is in my members.

I thank God through Jesus Christ our Lord. So then with the mind I myself serve the law of God; but with the flesh the law of sin.

### *Ephesians 1:6, 18*

To the praise of the glory of his grace, wherein he hath made us accepted in the beloved.

The eyes of your understanding being enlightened; that ye may know what is the hope of his calling, and what the riches of the glory of his inheritance in the saints,

# Exodus 28

## *Colossians 1:18*

And he is the head of the body, the church: who is the beginning, the firstborn from the dead; that in all *things* he might have the preeminence.

## *Revelation 1:13*

And in the midst of the seven candlesticks *one* like unto the Son of man, clothed with a garment down to the foot, and girt about the paps with a golden girdle.

## For Glory and for Beauty

Not mere tradition, outward duty
but a godly glory, beauty,
typified those priests of old
disheveled none, all clothed in gold.

Those Israelites, those sticks and stones
drawn out of Egypt, rags and bones,
now numbered of all humans, best,
now treasured on the High Priest's breast.

Yon Aaron being of Christ a type
a creature bearing human hype,
a plate of gold upon his head
in Christ alive, in Aaron dead.

Those sons of Aaron clothed as well
as Christian people, saved from hell,
all sanctified from head to toe
Christ came, Christ went—we rise, we go.

# Exodus 29

As Aaron's spiritual sons and daughters we are "lively stones . . . a spiritual house, an holy priesthood" who love to "offer up spiritual sacrifices, acceptable to God by Jesus Christ" (1 Pet 2:5). There has, of course, only been one Priest capable of fulfilling all the demands of God's holy law, and thereby completing the whole purpose of the original Aaronic priesthood; we walk in His shadow, the "garments", "ephod", "breastplate", "curious girdle", "mitre", "holy crown", "anointing oil", "coats", "girdles", and "bonnets" (Exod 29:5–9) all rightfully appertaining to our High Priest without Adamic origin.

We live in a given righteousness, one which we have not earned, "the robe of righteousness" (Isa 61:10) upon us if we are His. Despite the fact that our Father knows what we are going to say before we say it, and that He created us for His own purposes, and that we cannot for a millisecond get outside of Him in order to commune with Him as anything approaching an equal, even so with breath-taking condescension He calls *us* to "minister unto" *Him* (Exod 29:1), as if we could possibly be of benefit or grant pleasure to Him! Remember, it is *us* about whom He is speaking—the analogy of a man looking down upon a worm or a free man looking at a prisoner doesn't even come close to the reality that "from the sole of the foot even unto the head *there* is no soundness in" (Isa 1:6) us.

Strangers "shall not eat thereof" (Exod 29:33) because such things are holy, and they are "without Christ, being aliens from the commonwealth of Israel, and strangers from the covenants of promise, having no hope, and without God in the world" (Eph 2:12). If, for argument's sake, it could be imagined that a stranger might somehow enter into and start to partake of the holy things of God, he would promptly be discovered and cast "into outer darkness" where "there shall be weeping and gnashing of teeth" (Matt 22:13). Yet the Savior holds out the prospect of repentance and faith to the very end. If we will but speak to Him from the heart, seek Him with even the flicker of a broken and a contrite heart, He is ready to proclaim that "Today shalt thou be with me in paradise" (Luke 23:43), for "God sent not his Son into the world to condemn the world; but that the world through him might be saved" (John 3:17).

The key is the Cross, the altar foreshadowing it, for "whatsoever toucheth the altar shall be holy" (Exod 29:37). We must get to the Christ of the Cross, acknowledging His Lordship over us. We must reach out and by faith touch the hem of our holy Priest who alone can take away our sin. And once we have come to Him we must daily return "in the morning" and "at even" (Exod 29:39), looking unto our "continual burnt offering" (v.42) throughout the entirety of our pilgrimage, "for there is none other name under heaven given among men, whereby we must be saved" (Acts 4:12), and in a sense we are not one whit more saved with each passing day than we were the day we first crossed over and were consciously 'born again'.

These things are not just for our man-ward, horizontal benefit, although they are, but God's will is to so implicate Himself within us that He might "dwell among the children of Israel" and "be their God" (Exod 29:45) in the more active, quotidian sense. As Jews in "the spirit, *and* not in the letter" (Rom 2:29), our chief joy is to dwell where God is, and God is with His people, in their solitary communion and their corporate fellowship. We are to remind ourselves every day that we are a people who have been "brought" out of the slavery and deadness of spiritual "Egypt" (Exod 29:46). We are to rejoice not only in what God has done for us but ever more to meditate upon who He is, for "the everlasting God, the LORD, the Creator of the ends of the earth, fainteth not, neither is weary . . . *there is* no searching of his understanding" (Isa 40:28).

# Exodus 29

## VERSES UPON WHICH TO MEDITATE

*(ideally in each chapter's context)*

### *Isaiah 1:6*

From the sole of the foot even unto the head *there* is no soundness in it; but wounds, and bruises, and putrifying sores: they have not been closed, neither bound up, neither mollified with ointment.

### *40:28*

Hast thou not known? hast thou not heard, *that* the everlasting God, the LORD, the Creator of the ends of the earth, fainteth not, neither is weary? *there* is no searching of his understanding.

### *61:10*

I will greatly rejoice in the LORD, my soul shall be joyful in my God; for he hath clothed me with the garments of salvation, he hath covered me with the robe of righteousness, as a bridegroom decketh *himself* with ornaments, and as a bride adorneth *herself* with her jewels.

### *Matthew 22:13*

Then said the king to the servants, Bind him hand and foot, and take him away, and cast *him* into outer darkness; there shall be weeping and gnashing of teeth.

### *Luke 23:43*

And Jesus said unto him, Verily I say unto thee, To day shalt thou be with me in paradise.

## *John 3:17*

For God sent not his Son into the world to condemn the world; but that the world through him might be saved.

## *Acts 4:12*

Neither is there salvation in any other: for there is none other name under heaven given among men, whereby we must be saved.

## *Romans 2:29*

But he *is* a Jew, which is one inwardly; and circumcision *is that* of the heart, in the spirit, *and* not in the letter; whose praise *is* not of men, but of God.

## *Ephesians 2:12*

That at that time ye were without Christ, being aliens from the commonwealth of Israel, and strangers from the covenants of promise, having no hope, and without God in the world:

## *1 Peter 2:5*

Ye also, as lively stones, are built up a spiritual house, an holy priesthood, to offer up spiritual sacrifices, acceptable to God by Jesus Christ.

## To Minister Unto Me

Such holy clothes for sinful men
such holy oil for men of earth,
such priesthood ours perpetually
such love from Him eternally.

An altar sanctifying all
God's grace redressing sinners' Fall,
remember now the Mount of Law
to touch it meaning death for sure.

In tabernacle God would dwell
permitting worms' approach as well,
such condescension, loving care
to sinners born in Satan's lair.

The purpose of life—knowing God
no one can venture outside God,
in slavery we've had our being
redeemed in Christ we're done with fleeing.

# Exodus 30

IN ALL THESE BLESSED Tabernacle types and shadows of some 50 chapters in the Pentateuch, God's word encourages and reminds us New Testament believers that "we have an altar, whereof they have no right to eat which serve the tabernacle" (Heb 13:10). *They* means both those who were of the Old Testament age looking by faith to the ultimate Messiah, and also *they* who, professing to obey the Scriptures and having "the tabernacle of witness in the wilderness" (Acts 7:44), stubbornly limited their understanding to earthly types and would "not come to me, that" they "might have life" (John 5:40).

The chosen child of God sees Christ in every part of Scripture and rejoices in Him throughout it all. Even the "staves" (Exod 30:5) of this second altar of incense can remind us that we have a God who, as it were, moves with us throughout our pilgrimage and "will never leave thee, nor forsake thee" (Heb 13:5), but is available and accessible throughout all the earthly trials and tribulations He deems fit to set before us. The positioning of this second altar shows us how the believer's struggle is not now so much with the fear of hell as with the challenges of living a life of godliness and purity, offering up "the sacrifice of praise to God continually" (Heb 13:15), with contrition and supplication on a daily, hourly basis.

Our first role in life as priestly believers is not to deal with our selves or the world but to "minister unto" God "in the priest's office" (Exod 30:30) through our High Priest. Only after private devotion and consecration are we fit for anything else, be it personal, familial, or social. Without such personal communion we forfeit so much blessing, sanctification, and protection from on High. Yes our sin-natures have been dealt with at the brazen altar, and we have the "laver" (Exod 30:18) of God's word at our disposal. But no, without making further use of the means of grace we will not be contented

## Exodus 30

Christians, veering off like Lot into worldly-minded Sodom rather than like Abraham to the promised land of spiritually-minded blessing.

It is to the glory and praise of our High Priest that New Testament priestly-believers now only need their "feet" to be washed: "He that is washed needeth not save to wash *his* feet" (John 13:10), ie. there is an ongoing need for our walk to be purged from the dusty defilements of the day, as we are in but not of the world. However, in the days of the Tabernacle Messiah had not yet come in the flesh, and believers from the tribe of Levi were by their hands enacting and preparing sacrifices day by day and year by year, which prefigured Christ: "So they shall wash their hands and their feet, that they die not" (Exod 30:21). Christ by His hands fulfilled what we with ours could not, and so He once and for all brought to completion what the Tabernacle could but typify: "For Christ is not entered into the holy places made with hands, *which are* the figures of the true; but into heaven itself, now to appear in the presence of God for us" (Heb 9:24).

God the Holy Spirit renders us fit to minister unto Elohim, as seen by the "holy anointing oil" (Exod 30:31). He permeates all aspects of our dealings with God and man, and makes us to *be* "the temple of God" (1 Cor 3:16) through Christ. How dare we meddle with Him, seek to lower Him to the realm of smells, bells, or emotionally manipulative music, sullying the holiness and sanctity of God among us. We must not in any way "compoundeth" (Exod 30:33) our godly fellowship with lightness or an over emphasis on human personality. Nor must we monkishly seek to hoard Him and develop our own personal religion of escapist mysticism.

The specific instructions on how to worship God and what we should and should not be doing are plain for His children to see. Like Stephen preaching to the religious of his day, may we fear not the gnashing of teeth against us when souls feel convicted due to our lips and lives. May we show how wearisome and self-destructive it is to "always resist the Holy Ghost" (Acts 7:51); and may we be so "full of the Holy Ghost" that we have eyes only for "the glory of God, and Jesus standing on the right hand of God" (v.55). Scripture alludes not to any inherent tranquility or ability within Stephen, and so we too may actually seek to become less the stress-filled, anxious Christian and more the Spirit-filled, content Christian with "the face of an angel" (Acts 6:15).

Departures

## VERSES UPON WHICH TO MEDITATE

*(ideally in each chapter's context)*

### *John 5:40*

And ye will not come to me, that ye might have life.

### *13:10*

Jesus saith to him, He that is washed needeth not save to wash *his* feet, but is clean every whit: and ye are clean, but not all.

### *Acts 6:15*

And all that sat in the council, looking stedfastly on him, saw his face as it had been the face of an angel.

### *7:15, 44, 51, 55*

So Jacob went down into Egypt, and died, he, and our fathers,

Our fathers had the tabernacle of witness in the wilderness, as he had appointed, speaking unto Moses, that he should make it according to the fashion that he had seen.

Ye stiffnecked and uncircumcised in heart and ears, ye do always resist the Holy Ghost: as your fathers *did*, so *do* ye.

But he, being full of the Holy Ghost, looked up stedfastly into heaven, and saw the glory of God, and Jesus standing on the right hand of God,

### *1 Corinthians 3:16*

Know ye not that ye are the temple of God, and *that* the Spirit of God dwelleth in you?

*Hebrews 9:24*

For Christ is not entered into the holy places made with hands, *which are* the figures of the true; but into heaven itself, now to appear in the presence of God for us:

*13:5, 10, 15*

*Let your* conversation *be* without covetousness; *and be* content with such things as ye have: for he hath said, I will never leave thee, nor forsake thee.

We have an altar, whereof they have no right to eat which serve the tabernacle.

By him therefore let us offer the sacrifice of praise to God continually, that is, the fruit of *our* lips giving thanks to his name.

## A Perpetual Incense before the LORD

He glorified us through Himself
transcending once through holy veil,
pure gold and wood, God-man Himself
perfecting prayers which could but fail.

He justified us, rich and poor
bearing our sin outside the camp,
no soul worth less, no soul worth more
we all are lighted by the Lamp.

He sanctified us, sanctifies
our feet defiled by sloping selves,
He is our laver and our prize
into His word one washes, delves.

He lives beyond, we live below
in Spirit only can we cope,
for daily darkness brings us low
He—darkly through a glass—our Hope.

# Exodus 31

THERE IS A PALPABLE sense of completion as we near the end of Chapter 31. This is about as good as it gets BC; only the God-man could bring us into the momentous AD era. God's prophet—Moses, priest—Aaron, craftsmen—Bezaleel & Aholiab, between them would prepare a divinely ordained structure on earth, instructive for all succeeding generations of Jews until the time of Messiah who would fulfil its ultimate purpose and do away with its "weak and beggarly elements" (Gal 4:9). Notwithstanding, its moral proportions divinely etched into "two tablets of testimony, tables of stone" would endure for all time for they alone have been expressly "written with the finger of God" (Exod 31:18).

Thus, New Testament believers both "establish the law" (Rom 3:31) and fulfil "the law" (Gal 5:14) by living a life which is higher than any non-Christian can attain unto, through Christ who came not "to destroy, but to fulfil" (Matt 5:17). Later banished rather than welcomed into the very structure which was designed to lead us to Him, He "with his own blood, suffered without the gate" (Heb 13:12), leading us to "go forth" from all man-made religious establishments, nominally Christian or other, "unto him without the camp, bearing his reproach" (Heb 13:13). In an age of millions of Bibles, churches, and internet sermons, there is no lack of religion; however, the sobering reality is that true faith has and will become increasingly scarce so that "when the Son of man cometh, shall he find faith on the earth?" (Luke 18:8).

The days of apostasy and heresy in which we live are sadly adumbrated in Exodus 32, for after the conclusive references to eternal peace in which God "rested, and was refreshed" (Exod 31:17) there is a pre-emptive manifestation of "all deceivableness of unrighteousness" (2 Thess 2:10) in which God permits a large swath of supposed believers to fall into "strong delusion, that they should believe a lie" (v.11). The wretched impatience and ingratitude of much of this corporate body blessed in Moses with "a perpetual covenant" (Exod 31:16) is shocking. How could those precious instructions and promises of Exodus 31 so quickly deteriorate into the prayerless carnality of the "Up, make us gods" of Exodus 32!?

The echo is heard in our own day which is remarkably similar, for what culture has been more mightily transformed and blessed than the culture of Western Europe from the 16th to the 19th century? And yet what culture has been so hostile, arrogant, and disobedient to the things of God than Western Europe in the 20th and 21st century? In the last hundred or so years we have "sown the wind" of theistic and atheistic evolution, and are currently reaping the "whirlwind" (Hos 8:7) of societal breakdown, moral disintegration, and sexual perversion. We are so besotted with material abundance, never-ending technological advance, and financial gain, that when "in one hour" she is "made desolate" (Rev 18:19) we will be utterly devastated and distraught.

The real question is, what will endure on that mighty Day of Judgement? As believers in the crucified and risen Lord Jesus we are no longer preparing a foundation, for He is our "foundation" (1 Cor 3:11) upon whom we prayerfully build spiritual "gold, silver, precious stones" (v.12). If we prioritize worldly goals and triumphs then we may indeed attain them only to lose them at the end, being "saved; yet so as by fire" (v.15). We are to rejoice, moreover, in the fact that it is we ourselves who "are the temple of God, and *that* the Spirit of God dwelleth in" (v.16) us. In this sense it is not only the things which may come out of us which are to be prized and coveted, but the light of Christ who may be reflected through us. Just as an earthly parent desires the *presence* of his or her children as well as their gratitude, their love, their warmth of affection, our Father in heaven wants not just our gifts but *us*, for in Christ we are "chosen of God, *and* precious" (1 Pet 2:4).

Each one of us when alone for too long will become unreflecting and lonely. But as a blessed *ekklesia* of believers in Christ, we "are the light of the world" which constitutes "a city that is set on an hill", daring to testify of the light which "cannot be hid" (Matt 5:14).

Exodus 31

## VERSES UPON WHICH TO MEDITATE

*(ideally in each chapter's context)*

### Hosea 8:7

For they have sown the wind, and they shall reap the whirlwind: it hath no stalk: the bud shall yield no meal: if so be it yield, the strangers shall swallow it up.

### Matthew 5:14, 17

Ye are the light of the world. A city that is set on an hill cannot be hid.

Think not that I am come to destroy the law, or the prophets: I am not come to destroy, but to fulfil.

### Luke 18:8

I tell you that he will avenge them speedily. Nevertheless when the Son of man cometh, shall he find faith on the earth?

### Romans 3:31

Do we then make void the law through faith? God forbid: yea, we establish the law.

### 1 Corinthians 3:11-12, 15-16

For other foundation can no man lay than that is laid, which is Jesus Christ.

Now if any man build upon this foundation gold, silver, precious stones, wood, hay, stubble;

If any man's work shall be burned, he shall suffer loss: but he himself shall be saved; yet so as by fire.

Know ye not that ye are the temple of God, and *that* the Spirit of God dwelleth in you?

## Departures

### Galatians 4:9, 5:14

But now, after that ye have known God, or rather are known of God, how turn ye again to the weak and beggarly elements, whereunto ye desire again to be in bondage?

For all the law is fulfilled in one word, *even* in this; Thou shalt love thy neighbour as thyself.

### 2 Thessalonians 2:10-11

And with all deceivableness of unrighteousness in them that perish; because they received not the love of the truth, that they might be saved.

And for this cause God shall send them strong delusion, that they should believe a lie:

### Hebrews 13:12-13

Wherefore Jesus also, that he might sanctify the people with his own blood, suffered without the gate.

Let us go forth therefore unto him without the camp, bearing his reproach.

### 1 Peter 2:4

To whom coming, *as unto* a living stone, disallowed indeed of men, but chosen of God, *and* precious,

### Revelation 18:19

And they cast dust on their heads, and cried, weeping and wailing, saying, Alas, alas, that great city, wherein were made rich all that had ships in the sea by reason of her costliness! for in one hour is she made desolate.

## In All Manner of Workmanship


Whom God has filled cannot be killed
until God's work on earth is done,
no man can do what God has willed
outside of Christ, the Holy One.

For every saint Jesus atones
includes them in Himself, a part,
a spiritual house of lively stones
reflecting God in human heart.

As Jesus dwells each one indwells
feeling complete on Sabbath day,
those priestly pomegranates, bells,
resound above each church—Lord's day.

The Word of God to Moses given
put by God in stone, in table,
Adam, Eve, all souls have striven
with it, blessed, without—unable!

# Exodus 32

THE DOUBLE SENSE OF this rebellious, man-pleasing command ("make us gods" v.1) is surely intended, ie. *make*, and make *us* . . . for we not only want to worship what we want to worship, but we want to be the ones in control of what and how we worship, thus in a sense presumptuously take the place of God—so it was in the garden of Eden, so it is today. Rather than the simplicity of Bible teaching and prayer, religious man will have his cathedrals, his megachurches, his parades, his events, his arts, and his respected social status.

The worldly church of our day thus operates with the spirit of the golden calf, and the called-out believer must "come out from among them" and be "separate, saith the Lord, and touch not the unclean *thing*; and I will receive you" (2 Cor 6:17). This will at times be a lonely and a painful process, especially if it involves distancing yourself from those with whom you are emotionally close: "and slay every man his brother, and every man his companion, and every man his neighbour" (Exod 32:27).

Aaron's sadly misguided agenda is a warning to Christians today; negatively not to compromise, positively to submit all life's circumstances to prayer, thoughtful reflection, and at times uncomfortably honest biblical scrutiny. Moses had departed on his hallowed task for a season: "And when the people saw that Moses delayed to come down out of the mount, the people gathered themselves together unto Aaron, and said unto him . . ." (Exod 32:1). The people *saw, gathered, said*, without any reference to prayer, praise, and patient submission to Yahweh's providential delay. In our day churches can become impatient, the Gospel seemingly not reaching local communities, young people in congregations not being saved, pastors and preachers not as impressive as desired, especially when (unfairly) measured against a nostalgic golden age.

## Exodus 32

What to do? In this case the people hastily demanded liveliness and activity (*Up, make, go*). Why not, they thought, do as the Egyptians and use man-made methods to honor God. Aaron is sadly recorded as a warning to us: "And Aaron said unto them, Break off the golden earrings, which *are* in the ears of your wives, of your sons, and of your daughters, and bring *them* unto me" (v.2). What foolishness and confusion came upon them as a result of his accommodating, culturally engaged spirit. What foolishness and withholding of blessing will come upon those churches of our day, which meddle with worldly means and man-made culture in striving to honor God, according to a man-pleasing rather than God-pleasing agenda.

Meanwhile, those who refuse to dress down, loosen up, unbridle emotions, bring in popular lyrics, and befriend worldly-minded preachers may be depicted as negative, aloof, cold sticklers who are impeding the progress of the Gospel in modern times. Moses, by contrast, intercedes for God's people and by grace is permitted to bring about mercy when justice ought to have obliterated them: "And the LORD repented of the evil which he thought to do unto his people" (v.14).

Furthermore, Moses can be viewed as a type of Christ (the global Good Shepherd) and Aaron a type of New Testament church pastor (local under-shepherd). Aaron had union with God but in his moment of testing, his time of trial and peer pressure, he omits emergency prayer. After the outrageous and despicable demands of verse 1, Aaron's reaction ought to have been to call upon the Lord, pray to the Lord, turn his face towards the Lord and bring His righteous commands to bear upon those ungrateful, heedless rebels. Instead there is the dealing with the worldly-minded on their own terms: "And Aaron said unto them" (v.2); an immediate reaction rather than a prayerful pause: "Break ... bring" (v.2). How often have we, likewise, entered into a conversation or agreed to go along with a course of action without having resorted to the closet of prayer. I would suggest it is far more often than we might like to confess; if we are honest with ourselves, we have far more in common with Aaron than with Moses.

Aaron's response to Moses in terms of the typology of under-shepherd (pastor)—Shepherd (Christ) is illuminating. Instead of frank confession, open admission, repentance and renewed blessing, there is the spirit of Adamic blame and pathetic excuse: "thou knowest the people ... they said unto me ... and there came out this calf" (v.22–24). For our own sanctification we should see ourselves in Aaron; the original prayerlessness was bad enough, the subsequent muddled and inadequate confession worse. In the biblical context, the burden of leadership over a vast, mixed multitude of souls rather than a smallish, called-out, regenerate church membership was no easy thing. Modern elders, deacons, and members of churches live in less challenging times of "new wine . . . milk . . . waters, and a fountain" (Joel 3:18), in which the promised Messiah has become incarnate and has wrought an Almighty victory on the Cross.

However, the spirit of the golden calf is still with us, and the declension of the church can be traced to the same attitudes that false and compromised believers had in those days, which led to a situation whereby "the LORD plagued the people, because they made the calf, which Aaron made" (Exod 32:35). Similarly, "as many as I love, I rebuke and chasten: be zealous therefore, and repent" (Rev 3:19). Like Moses, our minds should be being increasingly consumed by the glory of God; unlike Aaron we should not be being swayed or blinded by peer pressure, not fearing the face of man, but zealously inclining our hearts both to hear and to apply the voice of God to modern church life: "He that hath an ear, let him hear what the Spirit saith unto the churches" (Rev 3:22).

# Exodus 32

## VERSES UPON WHICH TO MEDITATE

*(ideally in each chapter's context)*

### *Joel 3:18*

And it shall come to pass in that day, *that* the mountains shall drop down new wine, and the hills shall flow with milk, and all the rivers of Judah shall flow with waters, and a fountain shall come forth of the house of the LORD, and shall water the valley of Shittim.

### *2 Corinthians 6:17*

Wherefore come out from among them, and be ye separate, saith the Lord, and touch not the unclean *thing*; and I will receive you,

### *Revelation 3:19, 22*

As many as I love, I rebuke and chasten: be zealous therefore, and repent.

He that hath an ear, let him hear what the Spirit saith unto the churches.

## Make Us Gods

To Aaron Moses was as God
filled with the Spirit, full of zeal,
to Moses Aaron spoke for God
his mouth enabled to reveal.

Moses arose unto God's glory
Aaron sank with fear of man,
Moses' prayers were made revelatory
Aaron, prayerless, made his plan.

Moses, Christ-like, stood in between
God's wrath and sinners out of love,
God's name, God's glory he had seen
and yet descended from above.

Moses, like Paul, did wish to die
to save his people from their sin,
Aaron, like us, lived half a lie
to please the world, to save his skin.

# Exodus 33

HERE WE HAVE THE post-rebellion humbling of the Israelites whose "ornaments" (Exod 33:4), having been misused for false worship are now, albeit temporarily, put to one side. There is the notable absence of the beloved but compromised Aaron, and a sense in which the distinct, ceremonial forms of true religion will dissolve in the "cloudy pillar" (v.9) of *heart* religion with which all outward manifestations were designed to assist. God will go on to command His people to "rend" their "hearts, and not" their "garments" (Joel 2:13) while David, man after God's own heart, will confess in his terrible guilt that rather than "sacrifice" God desires "a broken spirit: a broken, and a contrite heart" (Ps 51:16–17). Thus throughout these earlier chapters of God-breathed revelation, we along with them are being purified and rendered more spiritual as we learn to lay aside earthly entanglements and outward ornaments in one form or another.

As God deigned to speak with Moses "face to face, as a man speaketh unto his friend" (Exod 33:11), so our Lord Jesus calls us "friends; for all things that I have heard of my Father I have made known unto you" (John 15:15). We are living in the fulfillment of much of Scripture which was progressive and anticipatory. *We* have unspeakable privileges and direct access to the throne of grace. God has promised to answer *our* prayers, solo Christo. We are builders now, whereas the believers in Moses' day were prophetic ground-breakers and preparers. The patriarchs, prophets, and apostles who "died in faith, not having received the promises, but having seen them afar off" (Heb 11:13) all did their divinely ordained duties so that we may reap what they sowed. We are even called a 'royal priesthood', 'his workmanship', and 'more than conquerors'!

However, there is something higher and more glorious than even our prayers and the gradual unfolding of the Jewish-Gentile international, global church of Jesus Christ. There is a higher quest, a watershed moment which demarcates the necessary pleadings and prayers leading up to verse 17, and brings us into the altogether more exalted realm of verse 18—the glory of God. How little it is appreciated, and how seldom our prayers begin where they ought; with God's glory, God's "goodness", God's "name" (Exod 33:19). As we hide our selves "in a clift of the rock" (Exod 33:22) of Christ, we may profit from a brief reflection upon each of His instructions as to how to approach our heavenly Father (Matt 6:9), so that we do not merely dwell at the base of the mountain of requests, pleadings, supplications, and confessions, but rise up in self abandonment to seek the pinnacle of prayer—a dwelling upon the attributes of Almighty God, a God who permits Himself to be identified, known, and loved:

"Our"—we may relate to God in child-like affection and exclusivity, for He is a God of "covenant" (Exod 34:10) and none other than God the Son, who "by himself purged our sins" (Heb 1:3), having "finished the work which" (John 17:4) only He could do.

"Father"—we may resort to God as the lover and discipliner of our souls, He who will protect and provide for us, for He is "merciful and gracious, longsuffering, and abundant in goodness and truth" (Exod 34:6)

"which art"—He is Self-sufficient. We have all had origination in earth and also in the divine mind before time began. He alone is "The LORD God" (Exod 34:6)

"in heaven"—He is spiritual. We are told in Isaiah that even heaven is but His "throne" (Isa 66:1), so He transcends all heavenly spirituality, as well as earthly comprehension. He "passed by" (Exod 34:6) Moses, for even the best of men cannot fully behold Him "and live" (Exod 33:20).

"Hallowed"—Separate, pure, holy. Everything we are not. "The LORD descended in the cloud" (Exod 34:5), for we cannot ascend to where He is, but must be lifted up by the Holy Spirit.

"be"—His being is wonderful, not merely in terms of creaturely realization by angels and humans but in Himself, before there was ever such a thing as a heaven or an earth, an angel, or a human. He is "The LORD" (Exod 34:6)

"thy name"—the sum total of all His attributes, or rather those attributes which can be perceived by us. If eternity were a thing ever to be completed (which it is not), it would still not be long enough to fathom the breadth, depth, and height of His name. God "proclaimed the name of the LORD" (Exod 34:5) to us; we did not and cannot discern Him except insofar as He deigns to reveal Himself.

With such thoughts in mind, may we become ever more sensitized to who He is, day by day, remembering that our heavenly Father has "provided some better thing for us" [New Testament believers], "that they" [Old Testament believers] "without us should not be made perfect" (Heb 11:40), and we "are all one in Christ Jesus" (Gal 3:28).

Departures

## VERSES UPON WHICH TO MEDITATE

*(ideally in each chapter's context)*

### *Psalm 51:16–17*

For thou desirest not sacrifice; else would I give *it*: thou delightest not in burnt offering.

The sacrifices of God *are* a broken spirit: a broken and a contrite heart, O God, thou wilt not despise.

### *Isaiah 66:1*

Thus saith the LORD, The heaven is my throne, and the earth is my footstool: where is the house that ye build unto me? and where is the place of my rest?

### *Joel 2:13*

And rend your heart, and not your garments, and turn unto the LORD your God: for he *is* gracious and merciful, slow to anger, and of great kindness, and repenteth him of the evil.

### *Matthew 6:9*

After this manner therefore pray ye: Our Father which art in heaven, Hallowed be thy name.

### *John 15:15*

Henceforth I call you not servants; for the servant knoweth not what his lord doeth: but I have called you friends; for all things that I have heard of my Father I have made known unto you.

## *17:4*

I have glorified thee on the earth: I have finished the work which thou gavest me to do.

## Galatians 3:28

There is neither Jew nor Greek, there is neither bond nor free, there is neither male nor female: for ye are all one in Christ Jesus.

## Hebrews 1:3

Who being the brightness of *his* glory, and the express image of his person, and upholding all things by the word of his power, when he had by himself purged our sins, sat down on the right hand of the Majesty on high;

## *11:13, 40*

These all died in faith, not having received the promises, but having seen them afar off, and were persuaded of *them*, and embraced *them*, and confessed that they were strangers and pilgrims on the earth.

God having provided some better thing for us, that they without us should not be made perfect.

## I Beseech Thee, Show My Thy Glory

A stiff-necked people, we as they
being all too keen to rise and play,
their ornaments caused them to stumble
so they left them, hearts to humble.

Tabernacle now without
the people plagued, their hearts drawn out,
for that which is too easy tempts
religious man to self attempts.

God's wrath was tempered, pacified
for Moses to himself had died,
his pleading for his brethren blessed
and yet one further, final quest.

God's glory dwelt in Moses' mind
to all the world becoming blind,
to know God's glory, one desire
self abandoned, seeking higher.

# Exodus 34

SCRIPTURE SPEAKS THROUGH SCRIPTURE, and reveals that "the law was given by Moses, *but* grace and truth came by Jesus Christ" (John 1:17), the "Prophet from the midst of thee" (Deut 18:15), which links all the way back to Genesis 3 and into the eternal counsel of John 17. We cannot fully appreciate the depth of human sin and necessity for a once and for all atonement *without* the Old Testament; and yet we cannot see the Old Testament as complete and fulfilled without the New. Thus, the transfiguration of Jesus in Matthew 17 is the definitive complement and conclusion to the merely reflected light of Moses in which only "the skin of his face shone" (Exod 34:30).

Man is a stubborn creature, and if the Old Testament were to have been extended to millions or billions of years (instead of thousands), we would still be unbowed and stubbornly clinging on to human works as the solution to our existential predicament, our way by which we may please God and enter into heaven at the end of time, on *our* terms. We cling to our own ways, thoughts, and works, especially in the realm of religion. We will not deal with God on His terms in which He deigns to save us 100% "by grace", 100% "through faith", 100% as "the gift of God" (Eph 2:8), not by anything which we can achieve through the mind or the body.

As Moses was, so are we to "be ready in the morning" (Exod 34:2) in order to commune with our heavenly Father in the closet of prayer. Our public face is not to be put on, as it were, until we have spent time in private with our "vail off", earnestly desiring "to speak with him" (Exod 34:34). A day in which we arise late and do not make time for private devotions, is a day which will not go well; we cannot be a blessing to others until we have first sought the blessing for ourselves.

We also find that the Bible sings to us in the Psalms, and in some ways this is where both Old and New Testaments meet. There it is that Moses steps back from his more immediate duties in order to reflect upon the LORD: "from everlasting to everlasting, thou *art* God" (Ps 90:2). His heart cries out for the Prophet, the Edenic Seed: "O satisfy us early with thy mercy" (v.14), who alone could usher in an era of unspeakable blessing in which "the beauty of the LORD our God be upon us" (v.17), an AD era in which *we* live!

We are the inheritors of such a song and so echo its words in a greater way, thus reflecting with more revealed knowledge the glorious work of the Holy One who atoned for our sins, rose from the dead, and reigns in glory—incarnate. He is the fulfillment of the "lamb" of Exodus 34:20, who enables us to see something of our stubbornness and inward depravity. He is, even now, writing His "epistle" through our daily lives, "written not with ink, but with the Spirit of the living God; not in tables of stone, but in fleshy tables of the heart" (2 Cor 3:3).

# Exodus 34

## VERSES UPON WHICH TO MEDITATE

*(ideally in each chapter's context)*

### Deuteronomy 18:15

The LORD thy God will raise up unto thee a Prophet from the midst of thee, of thy brethren, like unto me; unto him ye shall hearken;

### Psalm 90:2, 14, 17

Before the mountains were brought forth, or ever thou hadst formed the earth and the world, even from everlasting to everlasting, thou *art* God.

O satisfy us early with thy mercy; that we may rejoice and be glad all our days.

And let the beauty of the LORD our God be upon us: and establish thou the work of our hands upon us; yea, the work of our hands establish thou it.

### John 1:17

For the law was given by Moses, *but* grace and truth came by Jesus Christ.

### 2 Corinthians 3:3

*Forasmuch as ye are* manifestly declared to be the epistle of Christ ministered by us, written not with ink, but with the Spirit of the living God; not in tables of stone, but in fleshy tables of the heart.

### Ephesians 2:8

For by grace are ye saved through faith; and that not of yourselves: *it is* the gift of God:

## Behold, the Skin of His Face Shone

The breaking of the Law revealed
how in our hearts we had not heeled,
but worshipped that which was not God,
God's man pleading for man to God.

God's man hewed out two tables more
depending on God's mercy, sure,
the love of God being jealous, strong
God's man being zealous, God's in song.

The firstling of an ass redeemed
with creature blood, not manmade, schemed,
for stubborn, stiff-necked man conceives
aesthetic worship, heart deceives.

The hewing of the stone again
foreshadowed Christ's incarnate pain,
through Him the Law we do fulfill
through Him by Grace, our Father's will.

# Exodus 35

AS WITH SO MANY of the Pauline epistles, the divine pattern seems first to extol the glorious attributes of God, before instructing God's servants as to how to apply them to the trials and tribulations of everyday life. We may be greatly moved, for example, at the eternal plan of God revealed in Ephesians 1–3, before being challenged to live it out while on earth, in Ephesians 4–6. Such is the case in Exodus 35, in which all that has been revealed to Moses in Exodus 25–31 is henceforth to be put into practice. No good would it have been if God's people were simply to give themselves to passive mystical meditation; now is a time for holy action, a time for service, a time to search one's heart and see whether there be any inclination, any desire to do God's will "in earth, as *it is* in heaven" (Matt 6:10).

We are told that "the angels desire to look into" (1 Pet 1:12) the mystery of us earthen vessels being filled with the Holy Spirit, and God's unspeakable condescension in redeeming us mere creatures of clay. How is it that those rebel-hearted monsters of Exodus 32 could now be made "willing in the day of" God's "power" (Ps 110:3)? What a remarkable turnaround that such stubborn mules are now called out, one by one, to be rendered "wisehearted" (Exod 35:10). The Tabernacle would be constructed to instruct in so many ways, and of course to point to Christ who would be sought by the prophets of old who "inquired and searched diligently, who prophesied of the grace *that should come* unto you" (1 Pet 1:10); *you*, dear New Testament saint. Yes, you.

Moses therefore speaks God's words not merely for the people's wonderment but that they "should do them" (Exod 35:1). Not all would be privileged to give such offerings as "gold, and silver, and brass" (v.5). Some could not give any thing but their God-given skill of spinning goats' hair "with their hands" (v.25). We are not required to give *beyond* what we have, but are to give of what we *do* have with "wisdom" (v.26), from a "heart made

... willing" (v.29). Maybe it is that you are "poor in spirit" (Matt 5:3) and "mourn" (v.4) over your physical, mental, and financial inadequacies. No matter, for even your frail and inadequate prayers, if from a place of sincerity and love for Christ, are worth much in the sight of God who can make the "stones" to "cry out" (Luke 19:40), and who "formed man of the dust of the ground" (Gen 2:7).

Only those who are truly resting in Christ can work for God. Our souls on the weekly "holy day, a sabbath of rest to the LORD" (Exod 35:2) are to be re-set, as it were, that we may receive instructions and filter out distractions, becoming attuned to "the thing which the LORD commanded" (v.4). We are to be teachable and receptive to those who have been "filled" by our Father in heaven "with the spirit of God, in wisdom, in understanding, and in knowledge, and in all manner of workmanship" (Exod 35:31). We have not been left to our own opinions and devices as a faithful bride of Christ, but in multiple locations throughout place and time have been granted "some, apostles; and some, prophets; and some, evangelists; and some, pastors and teachers" (Eph 4:11). Such things have not been job opportunities seized upon by the arrogant and egomaniacal, but essential callings ordained by God "for the perfecting of the saints, for the edifying of the body of Christ" (Eph 4:12).

If Exodus 32 displays the best that man can come up with while temporarily abandoned to his wayward, idolatrous insanity, Exodus 35 reveals to us the meticulousness of God's approach to true religion, and speaks to us modern Christians in terms of shunning the organized chaos of seductive sensationalism in which the worldly specializes, and of seeking to do religious things "decently and in order" (1 Cor 14:40). God surely abhors the rock and pop, jeans and t-shirt approach of so much casual, carnal Christianity, for He "is not *the author* of confusion, but of peace, as in all churches of the saints" (1 Cor 14:33).

# Exodus 35

## VERSES UPON WHICH TO MEDITATE

*(ideally in each chapter's context)*

### *Genesis 2:7*

And the LORD God formed man *of* the dust of the ground, and breathed into his nostrils the breath of life; and man became a living soul.

### *Psalm 110:3*

Thy people *shall be* willing in the day of thy power, in the beauties of holiness from the womb of the morning: thou hast the dew of thy youth.

### *Matthew 5:3–4*

Blessed *are* the poor in spirit: for theirs is the kingdom of heaven.

Blessed *are* they that mourn: for they shall be comforted.

### *6:10*

Thy kingdom come. Thy will be done in earth, as *it is* in heaven.

### *Luke 19:40*

And he answered and said unto them, I tell you that, if these should hold their peace, the stones would immediately cry out.

### *1 Corinthians 14:33, 40*

For God is not *the author* of confusion, but of peace, as in all churches of the saints.

Let all things be done decently and in order.

## Ephesians 4:11-12

And he gave some, apostles; and some, prophets; and some, evangelists; and some, pastors and teachers;

For the perfecting of the saints, for the work of the ministry, for the edifying of the body of Christ:

## 1 Peter 1:10, 12

Of which salvation the prophets have enquired and searched diligently, who prophesied of the grace *that should come* unto you:

Unto whom it was revealed, that not unto themselves, but unto us they did minister the things, which are now reported unto you by them that have preached the gospel unto you with the Holy Ghost sent down from heaven; which things the angels desire to look into.

## Whosoever Is of a Willing Heart

To rest in God such privilege
to seek no self-ish sacrilege,
to be made willing to give up
to pour out self, a chosen cup

To be wise-hearted, knowing God
to want souls to be known of God,
to use your hands for God's glory
to turn away from man's story.

To be stirred up in mind and heart
to want to from this world depart,
to see the tabernacle's worth
to weigh the world and see its dearth.

To take much joy in Bezaleel
to pray that God through him reveal,
to learn from Aholiab's work
to serve servants, the Master's work.

# Exodus 36

HERE WE HAVE A proto-church, an organic, called out body of believers functioning as one, not *all* but specifically "every one whose heart stirred him up to come unto the work to do it" (Exod 36:2). There is now a unity and a harmony evident, just as "all the members of that one body, being many, are one body: so also *is* Christ" (1 Cor 12:12). Presumably there were many who did not share this spirit of gladness, who bitterly resented the onward march of Tabernacle construction, looking instead with irrational nostalgia at a supposed sense of ease and comfort offered by worldly Egypt. So it is with us today; we at times look at our energy, our money, our time, and wonder what life would be like if such things were *not* now increasingly devoted to the things of God, the interests of the local church. Shame on us when we allow such thoughts to be entertained, un-expelled.

The man of God, Moses, now "gave commandment" (Exod 36:6) that the abundance of giving of materials and resources be "restrained" (v.6). It is far from a problem in our modern, lukewarm age, but it is true that zeal in and of itself can become a stumbling-block, for there is such a thing as "a zeal of God" which is "not according to knowledge" (Rom 10:2). We are to get the wisdom of Christ at all costs, for "Wisdom *is* the principal thing; *therefore* get wisdom: and with all thy getting get understanding" (Prov 4:7); without it our church attendance and evangelistic activity might actually be doing more harm than good. Surely our Lord seeks quality over quantity, and "five words" of solid, Bible-based, clear communication are superior to "ten thousand words in an *unknown* tongue" (1 Cor 14:19) of emotional excitement and gushing sensationalism.

From Exodus 36:8 onwards the Lord chooses to efface human personality from view, foregrounding the specific beauty and symbolic significance of all the details of the Tabernacle, details which have already been conveyed but are of such importance. Who is Moses, after all, or for that matter the apostle Paul, but instruments of righteousness whereby we may be brought in our hearts to "glory in the Lord" (1 Cor 1:31). We are not to elevate heroes and champions of the faith above their stations, and certainly not to the detriment of honoring our heavenly Father. As the Holy Spirit from verse 8 refers to all the godly as *he* without distinction, so are we to "be perfectly joined together in the same mind and in the same judgment" (1 Cor 1:10) so that the particular human soul being used becomes of secondary importance, our faith standing not "in the wisdom of men, but in the power of God" (1 Cor 2:5).

The world of our day still thoughtlessly celebrates the pyramids of Egypt, the cathedrals of Christendom, and the temples of Eastern mysticism. It has no desire, no inclination for deep spiritual meditation upon the mysteriously specific instructions of "loops of blue" (Exod 36:11), "badgers' skins" (v.19), and "sockets of silver" (v.36). By contrast, "every wisehearted man" (v.8) is dwelling like a royal ambassador in the all sufficient "strong tower" of God's "name" (Prov 18:10). Like "an householder" he is seeking to bring "forth out of his treasure" of biblical study "*things* new and old" (Matt 13:52), for the edification of all who have been granted ears to hear, "in whose heart the LORD has put wisdom" (Exod 36:2).

DEPARTURES

# VERSES UPON WHICH TO MEDITATE

*(ideally in each chapter's context)*

### *Proverbs 4:7*

Wisdom *is* the principal thing; *therefore* get wisdom: and with all thy getting get understanding.

### *18:10*

The name of the LORD *is* a strong tower: the righteous runneth into it, and is safe.

### *Matthew 13:52*

Then said he unto them, Therefore every scribe *which is* instructed unto the kingdom of heaven is like unto a man *that is* an householder, which bringeth forth out of his treasure *things* new and old.

### *Romans 10:2*

For I bear them record that they have a zeal of God, but not according to knowledge.

### *1 Corinthians 1:10, 31*

Now I beseech you, brethren, by the name of our Lord Jesus Christ, that ye all speak the same thing, and *that* there be no divisions among you; but *that* ye be perfectly joined together in the same mind and in the same judgment.

That, according as it is written, He that glorieth, let him glory in the Lord.

### *2:5,*

That your faith should not stand in the wisdom of men, but in the power of God.

## Exodus 36

**12:12**

For as the body is one, and hath many members, and all the members of that one body, being many, are one body: so also *is* Christ.

**14:19**

Yet in the church I had rather speak five words with my understanding, that *by my voice* I might teach others also, than ten thousand words in an *unknown* tongue.

## For the Stuff They Had Was Sufficient

The world will hanker for success
craving contentment through excess,
but God through Moses limited
the human hand, high spirited.

Those hearts elect, wise-hearted souls
worked as one mind, no separate goals,
doing what God had planned to do
through chosen hands, in spirit true.

Although each one a soul unique
no self-glory did any seek,
so God the Spirit spoke of 'he'
as if each part were one body.

The Holy Spirit moved among
to animate each soul He'd strung,
to tune each brother by each brother
to God—glory, not another.

# Exodus 37

THE EXTENT TO WHICH acacia wood or "shittim wood" was used is notable in that it is reputed to be an extremely hard and durable wood, one which is not as prone as others are to rot and decay. However, wood is wood, and so when it comes to that supreme act of God forgiving sin there can be no wood of human merit involved, for "salvation *is* of the LORD" (Jonah 2:9). God's mercy was determined within the Godhead before time, the enacting of such mercy unfolding throughout time; through Noah's wooden ark, Tabernacle wood, ultimately Calvary's wooden Cross, all of which were purposed from eternity. Thus "pure gold" (Exod 37:6) rather than overlaid gold would be smelted down and used for such a regal purpose, and presumably a large percentage of all their available gold would have been reserved for this most hallowed, heavenly seat.

Bezaleel had the extraordinary privilege of superintending the construction of every element of this work, in accordance with the revelation given to Moses. Surely it was his destiny to be granted wisdom, skill, and knowledge in this regard. Surely, too, such ability could not be attributed to the learning and culture of Egypt, for not only was the Tabernacle radically different from anything the world had known, but presumably he would not have been allowed access to the elite Egyptian artisans and craftsmen of the day. The Lord's work, anyway, would not depend upon any worldly wisdom or expertise, "for ye see your calling, brethren, how that not many wise men after the flesh, not many mighty, not many noble, *are called*" (1 Cor 1:26).

We may at times wish that more artistic or scientific geniuses were called to the faith, but it is not God's normative way. The world may gawk at its Tutankhamun, its Sistine chapel, or its so-called *Christ the Redeemer* statue, but God's people are spiritually-minded and have a jealously protective love for the true and living "Christ Jesus, who of God is made unto us wisdom, and righteousness, and sanctification, and redemption" (1 Cor 1:30). Like Moses we refuse "to be called the son of Pharaoh's daughter" (Heb 11:24) but rather rejoice in being children of God, unsung workmen of His word.

The failure of false religion is that it gets stuck on particular objects or moments in time, becoming obstructive of that pilgrim spirit of progressive sanctification. The Jews of the New Testament were overly fixated upon "the gold of the temple" (Matt 23:16) rather than the more important implications of the "temple that sanctifieth the gold" (v.17). They were obsessed with the material "gift that is upon" (v.18) the altar rather than seeking to learn the lessons that were to be gleaned from "the altar that sanctifieth the gift" (v.19). Like a child at Christmas time we can be foolishly focused upon the wrapping paper of outward religiosity rather than properly receiving the true and saving gift of Jesus. We may even become more interested in church history than the very real and present danger facing dying souls around us, with whom we rub shoulders daily.

May we be granted eyes to see something of the supreme claims of Immanuel, so that we "count all things *but* loss for the excellency of the knowledge of Christ Jesus my Lord" (Phil 3:8); yes, all things, even the valid and worthy things of Christian heritage and faith-deeds of yore *if* they become obstructions to evangelistic outreach. May the insistent and repeated references to "rings" and "staves" in Exodus 37 remind us that nothing in this world is permanent, and that in a pilgrim spirit we are to "press toward the mark for the prize of the high calling of God in Christ Jesus" (Phil 3:14), for the end is closer today than it was yesterday. The time is hastening when "we shall all be changed, In a moment, in the twinkling of an eye" (1 Cor 15:51–52), so that nothing of materialistic fixation or emotional heartache will remain.

# Exodus 37

## VERSES UPON WHICH TO MEDITATE

*(ideally in each chapter's context)*

### Jonah 2:9

But I will sacrifice unto thee with the voice of thanksgiving; I will pay *that* that I have vowed. Salvation *is* of the LORD.

### Matthew 23:16–19

Woe unto you, *ye* blind guides, which say, Whosoever shall swear by the temple, it is nothing; but whosoever shall swear by the gold of the temple, he is a debtor!

*Ye* fools and blind: for whether is greater, the gold, or the temple that sanctifieth the gold?

And, Whosoever shall swear by the altar, it is nothing; but whosoever sweareth by the gift that is upon it, he is guilty.

*Ye* fools and blind: for whether is greater, the gift, or the altar that sanctifieth the gift?

### 1 Corinthians 1:26, 30

For ye see your calling, brethren, how that not many wise men after the flesh, not many mighty, not many noble, *are called*:

But of him are ye in Christ Jesus, who of God is made unto us wisdom, and righteousness, and sanctification, and redemption:

### 15:51–52

Behold, I shew you a mystery; We shall not all sleep, but we shall all be changed,

In a moment, in the twinkling of an eye, at the last trump: for the trumpet shall sound, and the dead shall be raised incorruptible, and we shall be changed.

### Philippians 3:8, 14

Yea doubtless, and I count all things *but* loss for the excellency of the knowledge of Christ Jesus my Lord: for whom I have suffered the loss of all things, and do count them *but* dung, that I may win Christ,

I press toward the mark for the prize of the high calling of God in Christ Jesus.

### Hebrews 11:24

By faith Moses, when he was come to years, refused to be called the son of Pharaoh's daughter;

## And He Made the Mercy Seat of Pure Gold

The beauty of the beaten gold
was more than mankind could behold,
because divinely carried out
it held no stain of human doubt.

The hardest wood was thus employed
for sinners were we, unalloyed,
till Christ in gold came in our form
to suffer wrath, clothe us, transform.

The rings were cast, each hollow space
transporting Christ from place to place,
or rather we by Him being led
as we the body, He the Head.

The man who guided human hand
was given grace to understand,
that all was glory, work divine
foretelling Christ,—old hearts' new wine.

# Exodus 38

WHAT WE VIEW AS being of high importance, what we daily reach for and prioritize; beauty, prosperity, status, are regarded by our Father as fit for only the lowliest of vessels for the worship of Him—"the laver of brass, and the foot of it" (Exod 38:8). In other words, the things which are so often highest in our minds, from a godly perspective are of the lowest priority in His kingdom. As the devil distracts and diverts, we can so easily become backward and ungodly in our thinking. The "Woes" of Christ, for instance, show how human foolishness had taken to valuing the "gold" or the "gift" more than the "temple" or the "altar", whereas from God's perspective the "temple" and "altar" were of infinitely more value than the various materials used as coverings, or the gifts placed upon them (Matt 23:16–21).

All such outward structures and objects associated with true religion are supposed to lead us to Christ. All the original things mentioned in Exodus 38 were eventually ransacked and destroyed; so too our own venerated cathedrals, churches, and chapels are so much earthy *matter* if they do not lead us to Christ. Even our cherished and most ancient of Bibles which are placed under lock and key in the museums of this world are products which become worthless pulp if they do not, by grace, lead us to Him. Rather, "Destroy this temple, and in three days I will raise it up" (John 2:19), along with all those who worship Him "in spirit and in truth" (John 4:24) who are "as lively stones . . . a spiritual house" (1 Pet 2:5), a fact which transcends the limits of human comprehension. We fail to learn this lesson at our spiritual peril, for all we decide to invest in which is not truly spiritual will come crashing down.

The various materials, substances, and properties of the Tabernacle all have special meanings and, as discussed previously, are worthy of further study and meditation. We may be impressed by the diligence and attention to detail exhibited by the selfless Bezaleel and Aholiab, men who were from different tribes but whose faith and God-given abilities were devoted entirely to the service of the Lord. They were not doing things for show; neither were they hanging back and adopting a stance of false humility as with Ahaz later on: "I will not ask, neither will I tempt the LORD" (Isa 7:12). In whatsoever sphere of Christian service we feel the Lord has put us in, may we do it wholeheartedly and zealously, doing it not merely in the name of a man or denomination but "in the name of the Lord Jesus, giving thanks to God and the Father by him" (Col 3:17).

We know that all denominational differences will dissolve upon that final day, and by grace we will be as the angels. However, while the earth still stands we have been set in nations, families, and local churches for our own good, so that a global Tower of Babel-like false religion won't be raised up to vaunt itself over us and block out the "still small voice" (1 Kgs 19:12) of God who works in relatively small bands of faithful, gathered believers. As in the Tabernacle where not a pin was out of place and all was in readiness to be moved on to the next phase of pilgrimage at God's command, we should desire to do our particular duties as well as possible, that we each may be called "a good servant . . . faithful in a very little" (Luke 19:17).

May we also hold nothing back, desiring to "cast in all the living" (Luke 21:4) we have if called to, being willing and generous with our time, money, and energy, all of which come from and glorify Him. Surely an attitude of half-heartedness or luke-warmness is abhorrent to our Lord and Savior, He who gave Himself for us. He elicits from our own lips a definition of the first four commandments of Godward worship: "Thou shalt love the Lord thy God with all thy heart, and with all thy soul, and with all thy strength" (Luke 10:27). Whether we are a giant of the faith or a little known widow, let us do all things to the utmost of our ability, soli Deo gloria.

DEPARTURES

# VERSES UPON WHICH TO MEDITATE

*(ideally in each chapter's context)*

### *1 Kings 19:12*

And after the earthquake a fire; *but* the LORD *was* not in the fire: and after the fire a still small voice.

### *Isaiah 7:12*

But Ahaz said, I will not ask, neither will I tempt the LORD.

### *Matthew 23:16-21*

Woe unto you, *ye* blind guides, which say, Whosoever shall swear by the temple, it is nothing; but whosoever shall swear by the gold of the temple, he is a debtor!

*Ye* fools and blind: for whether is greater, the gold, or the temple that sanctifieth the gold?

And, Whosoever shall swear by the altar, it is nothing; but whosoever sweareth by the gift that is upon it, he is guilty.

*Ye* fools and blind: for whether is greater, the gift, or the altar that sanctifieth the gift?

Whoso therefore shall swear by the altar, sweareth by it, and by all things thereon.

And whoso shall swear by the temple, sweareth by it, and by him that dwelleth therein.

### *Luke 10:27*

And he answering said, Thou shalt love the Lord thy God with all thy heart, and with all thy soul, and with all thy strength, and with all thy mind; and thy neighbour as thyself.

## Exodus 38

### 19:17

And he said unto him, Well, thou good servant: because thou hast been faithful in a very little, have thou authority over ten cities.

### 21:4

For all these have of their abundance cast in unto the offerings of God: but she of her penury hath cast in all the living that she had.

### John 2:19

Jesus answered and said unto them, Destroy this temple, and in three days I will raise it up.

### 4:24

God *is* a Spirit: and they that worship him must worship *him* in spirit and in truth.

### Colossians 3:17

And whatsoever ye do in word or deed, *do* all in the name of the Lord Jesus, giving thanks to God and the Father by him.

### 1 Peter 2:5

Ye also, as lively stones, are built up a spiritual house, an holy priesthood, to offer up spiritual sacrifices, acceptable to God by Jesus Christ.

## Of the Looking Glasses of the Women

Oh wretched human vanity
the self-regard, insanity,
the foot more fitting than the face
at least it knows its lowly place.

Oh cursèd man-made human ego
Babel's tower downed long ago,
and yet we want our selves to worship
humbled souls have God's friendship.

Oh cold and hardened human mettle
living for its precious metal,
silver, brass and gold as nothing
if our God does not us bring.

Oh outward, proud religionist
or brazen, smug revisionist,
remember well the widow's mite
Christ shows us up, showing her might.

# Exodus 39

THE GOLD, REPRESENTING THE everlasting, unchangeable nature of God, was not merely set aside and squirreled away as something not to be touched, but was permitted to be actively beaten "into thin plates" and "cut" into "wires" (Exod 39:3). It was to be intertwined with the symbolically blue, purple, scarlet clothing to be worn by the Aaronic priests. Such colors were not arbitrary or devoid of meaning. As C.W. Slemming has helpfully explained, such things reflect something of our glorious and ultimate Highpriest, Jesus Christ. Blue represents His Divinity, scarlet His blood shed for us wretched ones, and purple His ongoing role as priestly mediator between God and man.

Purple, being a composite of blue and scarlet (red) foreshadowed the blessed truth that *"there* is one God, and one mediator between God and men, the man Christ Jesus" (1 Tim 2:5). The infrastructure, furniture, and clothing associated with the Tabernacle was meaningless matter without that divinely incarnated one, the Lord Jesus. He it is who accompanied the Israelites throughout their wilderness years. He it is who came in bodily form at the appointed time, who died and rose again for sinners from all ages and places. He it is who goes with us when we go about our various evangelistic activities, whether a little Sunday school, or two inadequate believers knocking on doors in a local neighborhood. Immanuel, God with us, is intertwined with every jot and tittle of Scripture, for He alone wore the righteous "fine linen" (Ex 39:3) of a perfect, sinless life. No other patriarch, priest, prophet, or pastor can compare with Him, and the moments when we take our eyes off Him are the moments at which we spiritually decline.

Thus, when we have done all that we have done we leave everything at His feet, just as the Israelites of old "brought the tabernacle unto Moses" (Exod 39:33), Moses being a type of Christ. We assume nothing in our own right, claiming no inherent power or glory. To do so would lead to Fatherly judgement, the withholding of the Holy Spirit, temporary coldness, and spiritual fruitlessness. No, we leave all with our Savior and prayerfully await His will to be wonderfully worked out in one way or another. It may be that years of declension or lack of growth will come upon a faithful local church being threatened by treacherous wolves, or it could be that many souls like sheep will be shepherded in and saved as they sit under the sound of the Gospel. "Moses blessed them" (Ex 39:43) because they had done all things according to the word of God. However, it does not become immediately apparent *how* they were blessed, for there would be many years of twists and turns, ups and downs, failings and triumphs before Joshua, another type of Christ, would be permitted by God to lead them into the promised land of that time.

We too are not seeking an earthly kingdom, even in terms of substantial external growth and congregational expansion. Whether we be few or many in number, so long as we are faithfully abiding in Christ we will be blessed according to the perfect plan of the Omni-scient, Omni-potent, Omni-present One. Ultimately, this earthly and heavenly cosmos is going to have "passed away" (Rev 21:1), and there will be "the holy city, new Jerusalem, coming down from God out of heaven" (v. 2), and "God himself shall be with" (v. 3) His blood-bought ones permanently, no longer in a yet to be fulfilled way. There will be no more foreshadowing of things to come, no more deep and difficult symbolism, no more learned and painstaking study of Scripture, no more vaunting of human instruments or persecuting of God's children; no more will we utter the following prayer in faithful anticipation and expectancy, for there we will be, living it out in a perpetual present of everlasting blessedness:

> For thine is
> the kingdom, and the power, and the glory,
> for ever.
> Amen
> (Matt 6:13)

# Exodus 39

## VERSES UPON WHICH TO MEDITATE

*(ideally in each chapter's context)*

### Matthew 6:13

And lead us not into temptation, but deliver us from evil: For thine is the kingdom, and the power, and the glory, for ever. Amen.

### 1 Timothy 2:5

For *there is* one God, and one mediator between God and men, the man Christ Jesus;

### Revelation 21:1–3

And I saw a new heaven and a new earth: for the first heaven and the first earth were passed away; and there was no more sea.

And I John saw the holy city, new Jerusalem, coming down from God out of heaven, prepared as a bride adorned for her husband.

And I heard a great voice out of heaven saying, Behold, the tabernacle of God *is* with men, and he will dwell with them, and they shall be his people, and God himself shall be with them, *and be* their God.

## And They Brought the Tabernacle Unto Moses

Divinity, humanity,
entwined gold, purple, scarlet, blue,
for God moves through activity
not absent, distant, out of view.

Creation provides every need
if through it humans worship God,
for in the flesh we fell through greed
we're risen when we're born of God.

When work was done unto the Lord
they went to Moses, man of God,
when Christians by faith please the Lord
they live through Mediator, God.

And yet that tabernacle waits
for time when final saint is due,
and when that sinner thus abates
behold God's tabernacle—true.

# Exodus 40

WHEN ONE THINKS OF all the supposedly great things that the human race has accomplished throughout the rolling centuries: the pyramids, the Great Wall of China, the discovery of gravity, electricity, DNA, the words of Shakespeare, theories of Einstein, harmonies of Bach, men on the moon, and a thousand other sporting and cultural achievements, it is hard for a worldly-minded human to accept the following: "Verily I say unto you, Among them that are born of women there hath not risen a greater than John the Baptist . . ." (Matt 11:11)

In other words, the supreme achievement of the human race has not been the above-mentioned things at all, but rather the birth of a desert-dwelling holy man, one who preached difficult yet vital truths in a particular place and time. It is doubly hard for the worldly-minded to hear that ". . . notwithstanding he that is least in the kingdom of heaven is greater than he" (Matt 11:11). How unfair, common sense might think, how unjust that the kingdom of heaven is such an utterly superior and Other kingdom that no one on earth has any clue about it, no ability to attain it.

Such might have been the case with Moses. After all the arduous and momentous preparations had been achieved, after all the meticulous exactitude had been weighed, smelted, fashioned, carved, and assembled . . . to be shut out! But we know that this was not the case with Moses who, though not quite in John the Baptist's league, was supremely a man of God who sought with all his heart to do His will to the best of his God-given ability, which was considerable.

In terms of the wider chronology of the Pentateuch, we are hovering just before Leviticus 1:1, and are up to Numbers 9:15. And yet for a moment, it almost seems that human time stops and the Eternal presence, Shekinah glory, rips open the fabric of the space-time continuum and dwells awhile amidst the earthly accoutrements of human experience. The number of references in this final chapter to washing ("laver, water" v. 7, "wash them with water" v. 12, "put water, to wash" v. 30, "they washed" v. 32) is emphatic, though only God can inaugurate this divine construction for He will not share His glory with another; "yea, the heavens are not clean in his sight" (Job 15:15).

So it is in our daily Christian experience; there are times at which we step back or perhaps are arrested by the Holy Spirit, and realize something more "of him with whom we have to do" (Heb 4:13). It is true that in the new heaven and new earth we will be interacting with God in a very different, altogether more fulfilling and glorious way than at present; there will be no more saved-sinner, no more earthly-heavenly tension, no more fleshly, worldly, sinful pride; nevertheless, God is ever God, and even in our newly resurrected bodies we will only be able to take in so much, the secrets and mysteries of God belonging unto Him.

And so, "the glory of the LORD filled the tabernacle" (Exod 40:34) and indeed fills heaven and earth, and will fill the new heaven and new earth.

And there is nothing outside of God. Amen.

# Exodus 40

## VERSES UPON WHICH TO MEDITATE

*(ideally in each chapter's context)*

### Job 15:15

Behold, he putteth no trust in his saints; yea, the heavens are not clean in his sight.

### Matthew 11:11

Verily I say unto you, Among them that are born of women there hath not risen a greater than John the Baptist: notwithstanding he that is least in the kingdom of heaven is greater than he.

### Hebrews 4:13

Neither is there any creature that is not manifest in his sight: but all things *are* naked and opened unto the eyes of him with whom we have to do.

## And Moses Was Not Able

The Christian starts with Christ of course
then working outward in due course,
the tent assembled without fail
the precious ark hid by the veil.

The thief on cross went straight ahead
but most of us dwell on, not dead,
and so the holy furniture
is us in prayer's expenditure.

And then the laver there between
how dare we come to God unclean,
confess we must, in God's word plunge
our sins be cleansed, sin though expunged.

So Moses finished all the work
only to then outside it lurk,
as John the Baptist, leaping, knew
God's glory will make all things new.

www.ingramcontent.com/pod-product-compliance
Lightning Source LLC
Chambersburg PA
CBHW051056160426
43193CB00010B/1208